To Africa with a Dream

OLGA MARLIN

To AFRICA
with
a Dream

Scepter

Published by Scepter Publishers, Inc.
New York / Princeton, New Jersey
FIRST EDITION
ISBN 0–889334–69–3

Text composed in ITC Galliard fonts

Printed in the United States of America

To Blessed Josemaría Escrivá,
who made the adventure of my life possible

and

to my parents,
Hilda van Stockum and Spike Marlin,
who laid the foundations

Contents

Prologue

I stood on the busy Dublin quay watching the big ocean liner steam away to Canada—with my entire family in it! On this hazy, chilly September afternoon, I was engulfed in a loneliness so deep that I thought my whole life, and the world itself, would never be the same.

"What shall I do?" The question went around and around in my reeling mind, demanding an answer. The busy port pulsated with its own urgent life. People bustled to and fro, preoccupied with their own consuming concerns, but making no impression on me. They looked shadowy, like fleeting actors on some great stage, with me on the periphery. Alone.

Somehow I made my way back to the apartment and let myself in. It was comfortable, lovingly furnished by my parents; but the sight of the silent, solitary rooms broke my heart afresh, forcibly bringing back my longing for my family and for the familiar joys of the past. I flung myself onto the bed and burst into uncontrollable tears. I sobbed from the depths of my being, from an emptiness I thought nothing could ever fill.

Suddenly a gentle hand rested on my heaving shoulders. "Don't take it so hard, Olga," said my friend Therese Dwyer, who had quietly entered the room. "You'll be with them again soon enough—within a year's time, when you finish your studies."

I pulled myself up and looked at her through a mist of tears.

"No, Therese, I'll never live with them again. I know it." This from the depth of a conviction whose source I did not know.

"Nonsense," she said. "You're letting your emotions

run away with you. Anyway, you're nearly twenty-one, so it should be natural for you to want to leave home. I think you're just too attached to your family."

Never having thought of it from that angle, I was put on the defensive. "What do you mean?" I said. "What's wrong with loving my family?"

"Take it easy!" replied Therese. "I love my family too, but I don't want to stay with them forever. I want to lead my own life. You at least are very lucky—your plans are already made. You'll get your degree, become a teacher, and, who knows, maybe get a job near your family."

"There's more to it than that," I said slowly, trying to assemble the vague ideas of a lifetime. "I do want to be a teacher, but not just to get a job. I feel there's more to my life, perhaps even a calling to serve God in some way . . ."

How could I explain to her the confusion I was in, the emptiness I felt—an emptiness that my family had always filled, until these recent months when something akin to fear had begun to stir in the recesses of my being? Now my family had been torn away from me. Their departure removed the final fragile net from under my feet, and I fell into the dark hollowness within. But at the same time there was that inkling, a strong sense of God wanting something from me, something I had been searching for all my life.

Therese stared at me, her blue eyes looking startled. Never one to mince words, she demanded to know whether I wanted to become a nun. The comically disbelieving look on her face made my spirits lift a little.

"No, not really," I said. "I've looked into that, but for me it would be too confining. The world is a large place, and the truth of it all is that I want to be right in the thick of it."

"I heartily agree," said Therese, breaking into a merry laugh. "I must say, it wouldn't suit you at all."

"But there must be something, yet I haven't found it!" My unanswered questions, my still undirected longing for God, the departure of my family—the weight of it all came crashing down on my shoulders. "I feel as if my life has sailed away with my family and there's nothing left for me," I said, and again I broke down in tears.

Therese said bracingly, "What you need is a cup of tea." I followed her into the kitchen, comforted by her friendship, but hollow inside.

The future loomed dark before me with its unanswered questions.

1

Where It All Began

It was early October, in 1955. I was practicing the piano, partly to while away my loneliness, when I heard a rather hesitant knock on the door. I opened it, and standing there was a young woman with a round, friendly face, intelligent eyes behind gold-rimmed glasses, and, in contrast, a mop of short ginger curls on her head.

"Are you Olga Marlin?" she asked shyly.

"Yes."

"I'm Teddy Burke, a niece of Father John Costello."

"Oh!"

I remembered this priest friend of my mother's. When he had come over to say good-bye to my family, he had looked at me intently and said, "I have a niece who is doing something that I think would interest you." I had meant to follow that up, but with the trauma of my family's departure I had done nothing about it. I hadn't even asked the name of the niece!

"Come in," I said, feeling a little guilty. I led her across the living room to the armchairs in front of the fireplace. This was a Georgian house, one floor of which was occupied by me and another student, Gina Jackson. The autumn light streamed in through the long window.

"Uncle John told me about your family," said Teddy. "He thinks very highly of your mother. He told me she is Dutch and an artist, and also a convert to Catholicism. But you're Canadian, aren't you?"

"No," I replied. "I was born in New York, and the other five were born in Washington, D.C. We only lived in Montreal because of my father's job."

"What brought you to Dublin, then?"

"When I finished high school my father wanted me to

go to Trinity College, his old university, so the whole family moved here."

"What courses are you taking?" asked Teddy, her steady gray eyes alive with interest.

"I wanted to take Latin and English, but my Latin wasn't good enough, so I changed to French instead. After I get my degree next year, I hope to earn a graduate degree in education so I can be a teacher."

Teddy nodded. "I also studied languages and literature," she said. "I got an M.A. in English, French, and Spanish. I never thought of teaching, though. I don't think I would have the patience for it."

"What are you doing, then?" I asked.

"I help run a residence for women students on Northbrook Road. It's only just been started."

"Don't you live with your family?" I asked, surprised.

"My parents live in Sligo. My father is a retired doctor. I'm the youngest, and the other four all have jobs." She hesitated, and then added, "Perhaps I should explain that I belong to Opus Dei."

"What's that?" I asked. I'd never heard of it.

"It's a new institution of the Catholic Church, a way of holiness for the ordinary person in the midst of his or her daily work and social obligations. The founder is a Spanish priest, Monsignor Josemaría Escrivá."

"Holiness in the midst of work and social obligations?" This sounded strange to me. "How does it work?"

"It sounds complicated, but it's really quite simple. You do your work, whatever it is, as well as possible and offer it to God. That's what Opus Dei means: Work of God."

I thought about my studies for a moment in this new light, and felt uncomfortable, as I was not a disciplined student. I had never thought about looking for God in study, and I told her so.

Teddy laughed and said, "Few people do. I myself

didn't before I came into contact with the Work. How would you like to come see the residence where I live?"

"Now?" I was rather taken aback by that immediate decisiveness.

"Why not, if you're free?" she asked.

Why not indeed! To my own surprise, I found myself accepting the invitation.

So we mounted our bikes, rode together towards Leeson Park and Northbrook Road, and pulled up at the front of a large ivy-covered Georgian home. Teddy opened an iron gate and we climbed steep steps to an arched porch, where Teddy rang the bell. The door was promptly opened by a motherly-looking young woman with dimples, fair hair, and gentle blue eyes. Her face warmed when she saw us. "Come in, come in!" she said, and guided us into the foyer. Teddy introduced me: "Maire Gibbons, this is Olga Marlin." We shook hands, and Maire took my coat. Then she asked, "Would you like to see our oratory?"

I was already familiar with the layout of the rooms, as it is the same in all Georgian houses. So when Maire opened the door to what I thought would be the dining room, I was amazed to see there an altar, with tabernacle, under a large mahogany-framed painting of the Madonna and Child. These young women actually had our Lord living with them in their own house. I couldn't believe it!

After that they led me to the large, high-ceilinged living room next door, invited me to sit down, and then went away. I could hear noise and laughter coming from below, and a short time later Maire returned with three other young women. In a flurry of introductions I met Anna Barret, Carmen Torrente, and Beatriz Montserrat. Carmen and Beatriz were both from Spain. Maire said, "I'm so sorry we left you alone, but Teddy has just found out that she's going to Rome, and she's trying to get herself organized!" Before I left, Anna asked if I would like to come there for Mass in the mornings. I liked the idea, because I found the little oratory invitingly intimate and the girls welcoming.

I asked Therese to come with me, and she agreed to. Therese was impressed by the atmosphere of the house, its inviting simplicity. "It's like a family, they're all so warm and friendly," was the way she put it.

Maire, who had a degree in home economics, managed the kitchen, and she invited me to come whenever I could to give her a hand. It was much more pleasant at Northbrook than in my apartment, since Gina was out most of the time and I was used to having my family around me. I soon made a habit of coming after school to Northbrook, to the warm and cozy kitchen, where Maire always had something for me to do. She wore an impeccable white smock and worked skillfully, rolling pastry, basting meat, or preparing steamed puddings, with me chopping the carrots or shelling the peas, while we talked.

"My mother is a vegetarian," I told her, "so we always ate lots of raw fruit and vegetables at home. She called this kind of diet '*roh kost*,' which is German for 'raw food,' and sometimes we went for days on nothing else. There was always a big bowl of muesli on the table. Muesli is made of fruit and condensed milk . . ."

As I said that, I remembered with a pang the sight of my mother's hands happily grasping one fruit after another to generously grate or slice into the bowl. "The best part of the apple is the core!" she would remind me, dropping it into the bowl with a flourish. Mother had a wholesome, down-to-earth appreciation of everything natural.

"Oh, show me how to make it!" Maire exclaimed, fascinated. So the next day I came with all the ingredients and we made muesli for tea. When the others picked their way down the narrow stairs to the cheerful basement dining room with its big round table and red-and-white-checked mats and napkins, they looked at the bowl suspiciously and then gingerly helped themselves to what they called "mush." Maire loyally filled her plate with it and pronounced it delicious. I suppose I had some way to go before reaching my mother's perfection!

I soon felt at home at Northbrook. It was lovely to arrive on cool, wet autumn evenings to find welcoming lights in the windows and Carmen sewing in the "green room," the only small parlor in the house. One day, as I sat watching her slender fingers deftly leave invisible stitches in the material on her lap, she confided to me, "I like to work in this room because that way I can greet the girls as they come in. They are always full of stories to tell."

On my visits I noticed that the oratory seemed to be the most important room in the house. Everyone stopped there a moment when going out or coming in. Once a week the chaplain, an Opus Dei priest named Joseph de la Torre, gave a talk there for residents and friends. I started to attend.

When I began asking Carmen questions, she lent me a book called *The Way*, by the founder of Opus Dei.

"How do you like it?" she asked when I returned it some days later.

"I like it very much," I said. I remained quiet for a little while, and then voiced the real question on my mind. "But how does a person know if she has a vocation?"

"It's something that God puts into the heart; nobody else can give it to you. It's a restless feeling that God wants more, and a desire to respond, though often that is accompanied by fear, because it means a commitment."

"Do you join Opus Dei forever?" I was young, and forever seemed a very long time.

"Yes, it's a lifetime commitment."

A lifetime commitment. I thought about that for a while.

"Then what difference is there between this and a vocation to religious life?" I asked, rather puzzled.

"The same difference that there is now between you and a religious. People who join Opus Dei don't leave the world. They remain where they are, in their studies, job or profession, and place in life. Opus Dei gives them the spiritual guidance they need in order to fulfill the commitment they make to strive for holiness, living their Christian life to the full, practicing virtues, fulfilling the duties of their state in life. There are all kinds of people in Opus Dei—married and single, young and old, sick and healthy."

I thought about what Carmen had said: that a vocation is something God puts in the heart; something no one else can give you. I remembered how every school day in D.C., from when I was six till I was ten, we regularly filed past a life-size statue of the Child Jesus in the school corridor. His feet were bare, and one hand was raised with two fingers held out in a teaching gesture, while on the other was an open book on which was written:

"If you   Come fol-
love Me   low Me."

As I was just beginning to learn to read when I first saw it, the hyphenation fascinated me and the words impressed themselves on my mind, together with that association of love for God with the intimate friendship of being a disciple. After a time those words had taken on the quality of a personal invitation.

One morning Maire looked particularly pleased when she opened the door. "A very important priest is celebrating Mass for us today," she said. "He is one of the first three priests of Opus Dei and is on a visit to Ireland." I was duly impressed. When Mass was over, I was introduced to him in the foyer. Father José María Hernández Garnica looked at me quizzically from behind dark-rimmed glasses as we shook hands. He had a very high forehead, with graying hair combed backward. "So you're Olga," he said with a smile.

Before I headed out to the college, Maire asked me, "Can you come around this evening for a chat?"

I wondered what she had in mind, since she sounded a bit formal, but I said, "Yes, I can come after dinner." I felt nervous, because I had flitting through me the sensation that things were coming to a head. I trod the well-worn cobblestones of Trinity's front square as usual, going from class to class, but inside me everything was just a thick, dense cloud.

When I knocked at the door of Northbrook Residence that evening, Maire was there waiting. "Let's go to the green room," she said, leading the way, and there we sat down together on the sofa.

"Olga," she said, without preliminaries, "I want to ask you something. Have you ever thought that you might be called by God to Opus Dei?"

I hadn't faced that question squarely, though I knew it was waiting to be asked. "What would it mean?" I asked, stalling.

"The women of Opus Dei who join like me are called numeraries. They remain unmarried in order to belong only to God and to be totally available for the apostolic needs of the Work." I understood that. It was the idea I had of a vocation. But was it for me? Was it what I had been hankering for, without knowing it?

Her look was affectionate and inviting as she actually put to me the question: "Olga, would you like to join Opus Dei?"

In these words I heard the call, the something more that God wanted of me. All the pieces of my life came together. The fears and uncertainties of the last months finally resolved themselves in my mind.

"Yes," I said, my mind perfectly clear.

Then I asked, "What do I have to do?"

Visibly moved, she answered, "You write a letter to the founder asking admission to Opus Dei as a numerary member."

"I didn't bring anything to write with," I said. When Maire went in search of paper and pen, this gave me time to consider what I was about to do in response to the call that our Lord had finally made plain to me. I experienced a deep inner peace at being able at last to answer "Yes."

Before leaving the house that night, I went into the oratory. It was in darkness, the flickering of the vigil lamp casting shadows around the room. I prayed there a while, with a heart full of gratitude.

* 2 *

Finding My Feet

After that I threw myself into my new family. The day after I wrote my letter I stayed to talk with Anna, the director, so that she could start explaining to me, little by little, the different aspects of the spirit of Opus Dei. She told me how I could jump out of bed at a fixed time in the morning, offering God the "heroic minute," telling him I was ready to serve. The following morning, while it was still dark, I scrambled eagerly out of bed after a quick look across the room at Gina, who was still asleep. I felt quite zealous then, though later there would be days when jumping out of bed would be much harder and therefore truly heroic.

When Therese returned from a trip to England and I told her what I had done, she was upset. She said, "Olga, can't you ever do anything by halves?" She continued to come with me to Northbrook in the mornings, and I longed for her to have a call like mine. I tried to talk her into it, but Therese's was another way. She had already met her Geoffrey. Eventually they got married and left Ireland.

I continued to meet regularly with Anna. Her big, shining gray eyes widened in a warm welcome whenever I arrived, and always she was ready to listen to me. I wanted to be like Anna. She seemed so selfless, always serene and smiling, and I thought she must be very close to God.

She helped me get my life organized. "God comes first," she said, "so you need to plan the times you will spend with him every day. They are appointments with God, and he shouldn't be kept waiting." First came the Morning Offering, which is essentially a resolve to live the coming day with God, for God, and in awareness of the presence of God, despite the big and little setbacks that inevitably will arise.

Then, in private prayer, one placed oneself before God and spent time with him. Some days one had a lot to say; other days, little or nothing; but one loyally presented oneself, as in any good friendship, to talk and to listen to the Friend.

"Study is an important part of that plan," said Anna. "Sanctifying one's study includes striving to make good grades, and that means hours of concentrated effort, offered to God, every day." I still found this quite novel, but I dug in with enthusiasm.

So my lifestyle at Trinity College changed. I studied more and went out less often for coffee and the flicks. One afternoon as I was riding out the front gate on my bike, a young man stopped me. "I've noticed you in the study lounge," he said earnestly, "and I would like to get to know you." My heart skipped a beat—how many times I had dreamt of a moment like this!—and then I hastily told him, "I'm already engaged!" and rode off.

In one of our conversations Anna asked, "Have you ever been enrolled in the scapular of Mount Carmel?"

"Oh yes!" I said. "Mother had us all enrolled when we were in Montreal. One cold winter's day I came home from school to find her waiting impatiently at the door with the little ones already bundled up to go outside. A taxi was waiting, and Mother scooted us all in, saying, 'I'll explain on the way.' She directed the French-speaking driver to take us to the Carmelite convent, and then she said, 'I read today that our Lady wants us to wear the scapular of Mount Carmel, and that she promises her special protection to all who do.' She then told us about all the blessings the popes have attached to the wearing of the scapular and why she couldn't put off getting us enrolled.

"The Carmelite convent was in old Montreal, and the

driver got lost, so it took us all evening to get there. When we finally arrived, the taxi driver, impressed by all that he had heard, insisted on being enrolled too."

Anna looked amused. "You must have a wonderful mother," she said.

One evening after dinner, while we were chatting together around the fire in the living room of Northbrook, I announced, "On November 12 I'll be twenty-one." Everyone sat up. "What?" "Why didn't you tell us before?" "Now we'll have to give you a key to the house!" Then Anna asked, "What do you usually do on your birthday?"

How could I begin to explain what birthdays meant in our home? From as far back as I could remember, they were filled with wonderful traditions.

"A birthday is a very important event in my family," I said. "As children we vied with one another to be the first to find 'God's present,' which could be a snowfall, a frost picture on a window, a beautiful sunrise . . . The birthday child politely thanked God, while waiting for more tangible things. The rest of the family gathered in a semicircle at the dining room door, each holding a gift, and then the birthday child was called and self-consciously came down the stairs while everyone sang 'Happy Birthday' and my Dutch grandmother—Mother's mother, who lived with us—continued with 'Lang zal ze leven . . . Hip, hip, hurray!' It was exciting to open all the presents before hurrying off to school with a bag of candy to share with the rest of the class. In the afternoon we had a party, for us and our friends, which included a birthday cake with candles."

"How did your mother manage to put all that together every year for six children?" exclaimed Beatriz.

"She loved to make us happy. 'No one remembers the ordinary days,' she would say, 'but special days are never forgotten.' So she skimped on the first and lavished on the second. After all the excitement was over, she would come to our room to kiss us good night. Those were special moments when my sister Brigid and I would exchange confidences with her. She called us boa constrictors, because we clung to her so and wouldn't let her go."

On the morning of November 12 I arrived at Northbrook as usual, and Anna met me at the door with a big smile. "Happy birthday!" she said in a low voice as we made our way to the oratory. "The priest is offering the Mass for you today."

I was the last to come out when Mass was over, and there in the corridor, forming a semicircle, stood everyone in the house. As soon as I appeared they began to sing enthusiastically, "Happy birthday to you . . ." and afterwards I was showered with hugs and congratulations.

"You must make sure to be back by six this evening," Anna told me, and I promised I would.

When I arrived she was waiting for me in the foyer, alone. The house seemed very quiet. "Perhaps we should go downstairs," she said mysteriously, moving in that direction. I followed her down the steep steps to the basement. There she went to the door of the family room, hesitated a moment, and then knocked hard and called out, "The birthday girl is here!" Instantly the door flew open, and in the midst of the surrounding darkness twenty-one candles burned on a magnificent birthday cake, their light reflected on the beaming faces of María Teresa Valdés, Maire, Carmen, and Beatriz, who all sang with gusto, "Happy birthday, dear Olga, happy birthday to you!" I looked around at them all, and then at Anna, who stood beside me smiling, and thought what a wonderful family I had found.

Not long after, Anna read out a letter from Rome asking us to pray and work hard for funds for the construction going on at Villa Tevere, Opus Dei's headquarters, backing up the titanic efforts of the secretary general, Don Alvaro del Portillo.

"One way we can help," Anna said, "is by cutting down as much as possible on our own expenses." I knew there wasn't much to cut down on, since, although everyone pitched in all her earnings, Northbrook was already running at a deficit and things were very tight.

"If we ration the lights," suggested Maire, "we can save on electricity."

"I'll turn your skirts inside out so they look like new," promised Carmen, while Beatriz came up with the idea of giving private Spanish lessons. I was still a student and could only contribute the pocket money my parents sent.

One day I did a foolish thing. I cycled through the city with an envelope in my coat pocket containing the apartment rent my parents had sent. When I arrived home I found it was gone. I couldn't believe it—twenty pounds lost when we were so bad off! I set out on foot and searched high and low, but the envelope was nowhere to be found. Instead of contributing to Northbrook I had to ask the others to replace my rent money. I met with nothing but sympathy and understanding, but it was a bitter experience.

"Tomorrow is the feast of Saint Nicholas," Maire said that day. "He is Opus Dei's intercessor in heaven for financial matters."

I was glad to know that. Saint Nicholas had always been an important personage in my family. We followed the Dutch tradition of celebrating Saint Nicholas' Eve (December 5). My parents created an atmosphere of anticipation and, in their grown-up conspiracy, produced a wonderful great Saint wearing a white gown, a red cloak, and a gilded miter. As he sat down in the special chair reserved just for him, with all of us children dressed in our Sunday best, he would take out his book and run his finger down the page, calling out our names one by one. As we each took our turn before him, he gave us an admonition to be good, and a wrapped present to open. When we were once again seated on the white sheet spread on the floor, he would stand up and, reaching into a small bag, shower us with handfuls of chocolates and other candies, which we scrambled to grab. When we looked up, he would be gone.

Now I would continue to go up to Saint Nicholas, but this time to ask him for money instead of candies. Little did I realize then how frequently I would have to appeal to the Saint over the years, sometimes desperately, for the funds needed to finance the many projects I would be involved in.

I wrote to Mother telling her about Opus Dei and my desire to join it, and she replied asking me to talk to Father Pius, her Carmelite confessor on Clarendon Street, which I did. I felt nervous about it, as I didn't know how to explain to him that I had a calling but not to religious life. We sat at a table in the visiting room and he listened carefully while I told him what I was doing. Then he encouraged me, saying at the same time, "Be sure and keep your parents informed."

I wrote long letters to them, and in May told my mother that I had been admitted to the Work. I also asked if I might keep the piano and the furniture from the apartment for Northbrook Residence, now that I intended to go live there.

Mother's reply from Montreal was not long in coming:

> . . . Since God has arranged things so that I can't come to you this spring, I see very clearly that his will is that you take this step by yourself. Whatever God decides is what I want. God will have wonderful plans in store for us.
>
> It's a funny thing, I find that I am far from all my children except Liz. There must be a reason for it and I'm not complaining. I would rather this than to have you all beside me. I want you to serve God and bear fruit. . . .

The fact that you have been able to take this step makes me very proud of you. I would like to think that I didn't have you too much attached to me. . . . Do you remember that was what people said?

I will come to see you as soon as I can. The piano is yours, of course. I thought you were going to come here, and in that case you would have had to sell it, but I give it to you with all my heart. Tell me what I can do to help you, and what you need.

Tell me more about everything. I am glad to have this chance of proving something that I have always believed: that my children don't belong to me, I have them only on loan. . . . I was deeply convinced of this, and now I give thanks because you have found your way.

Receive my blessing. Don't worry about me in the least. The one who is going to feel it is your father; I have to pray for him. I have already written to tell him that you have given your life to God in Opus Dei.

I read what you wrote to me, that I am the one who taught you to put God first. . . . I think that, in a way, I share your vocation. We are together, and isn't it wonderful?

Well, darling, words are not needed. I am with you a hundred percent.

Nothing more.

Hugs,
Mom

Over the years I have had reason to value and deeply appreciate the constant support my parents and the rest of my family have given me along the path I chose to take. But at the time I was disappointed to find that many of my parents' Irish friends were not so under-standing. It was difficult for them to appreciate a dedica-tion to God that didn't fall within a familiar framework, which for hundreds of years had been to move away from the world, and they were wary about it. The idea of living out a vocation of intense friendship with God in the midst of the world seemed strange to them, although it had been the norm in the early days of Christianity. All those early Christians—slaves, patricians, soldiers, parents, children—lived an impressive sanctity, often to the point of martyrdom, though they were ordinary people with nothing special about them. This truth, once self-evident, had since been forgotten.

* 3 *

A Teacher at Last

One day when the family was still living in Dublin, my father took me out with him—just me. I was thrilled. Daddy traveled a lot on business, and his visits home were frequent but short. Now he wanted us to have a whole morning to ourselves. On this occasion he wanted to discuss careers and open up horizons for me, though at first I didn't realize it. As we drove around the city, it was evident that he wanted to share with me more of his life. I asked many questions, and enjoyed our intimate conversation.

At last he gave me a shy, searching look and asked, "Olga, why don't you think about studying to become a psychologist or a psychiatrist, since you're so interested in people?"

I hesitated before answering. I knew my father wanted the best for me, but I had long since determined to become a teacher. No other career appealed to me. I told Daddy I could never be anything but a teacher. I felt very strongly about this. I'd always thought that teaching was a matter of self-giving—in fact, a kind of vocation. Daddy obviously had something else in mind for me, but he respected my decision. He was a good father.

I had discovered this vocation at the age of nine. We children were quarantined at home in D.C. because Brigid had scarlet fever, so I decided to play school and teach my brothers and sisters. I dressed up in Mother's clothes to look grown up, and they were quite impressed and cooperative. We set up a class schedule, and I taught them all I could. Mother commented that I was a good teacher, and I felt so encouraged, and had found it so fulfilling, that I made up my mind then and there to be a teacher when I grew up.

Years later Mother confided to me that she had sometimes worried because she felt she wasn't a good disciplinarian, but that when she told the priest about it, he said, "You're doing a rare and extremely important thing—letting your children be themselves."

Mother liked to write family stories, and she would read them out to us so we could make our comments. Afterwards she would say, "You are my best critics." She also painted, and Daddy set aside the brightest room in the house for her studio. None of us escaped hours of "sitting"—sometimes bribed with money—and the walls of the house were covered with paintings.

I shared Daddy's enthusiasm for watching Mother paint. I loved seeing essences gradually appear on the canvas as she put in stroke after stroke of her brush with infinite care, her little finger resting lightly on the canvas, palette in the other hand. Absorbed in the subject she wanted to portray, she brought out its inner beauty, and I saw people and things with new eyes.

"I can't paint what I don't love," Mother told me, and this was apparent in her portraits. It was fascinating to see the person come alive on the canvas, especially the eyes, which she sketched in first. She painted the *person,* and seemed to see each one with the love with which God sees them, bringing out their best.

———

At the end of the 1955–56 school year I graduated from Trinity College. Everyone at Northbrook made a fuss over me, and I was touched to find Carmen carefully ironing the rented hood and gown. Usually no one bothered to iron graduation gowns. The imposing Examination Hall was hung with solemn portraits of the university provosts, including my mother's Irish great-grandfather, Richard MacDonnell. The hall was presided over by a large stained-glass window and was alive with color as the procession made its way towards the stage.

Anna, Maire, and Beatriz were there to clap for me when I went up to receive my diploma. At home we celebrated with a treat prepared by Maire.

I registered at University College for the graduate program in education because, it being a Catholic university, I thought it would be easier to find there other girls with whom to share my newfound ideal.

On the first day of the semester I felt like a new girl in grade school. I missed the familiar environment of Trinity and all my friends. Here, knowing no one, I stood helplessly on the steps of the main building, wondering where to go. I was rescued by a big dark-haired girl who was talking animatedly among a group of friends. She caught sight of me and immediately came over.

"Are you new here?" she asked, smiling. "Yes," I replied, smiling back gratefully. "I'm Margaret O'Leary," she said. "What's your name?"

I told her, and then explained that I was looking for the graduate-level classes. "Come, I'll show you," she said. "I know where you need to go. We can have a cup of coffee afterwards."

Margaret and I often met in the college cafeteria after that, and became good friends. "My father is a wonderful person," she told me. "He's a policeman, and so dedicated to his work. I'm planning to get a job in a business firm, but at the same time I also want to serve God." I told her about Opus Dei and the idea of sanctification of work, and she was interested. She visited Northbrook and before long was coming for the weekly talks.

We went together to listen to a lecture given by Dom Eugene Boylan, a famous Benedictine monk, in the University College chapel, Saint Stephen's Green. He was a powerful speaker. One thing he said was, "Nowadays there is no easy way to heaven. In the past, when the entire Western world was Christian, a person could expect to get there with a minimum of effort, supported by everyone else. It's not the same today. The world needs saints and nothing less will do. Heaven can be compared to a great theater where all the less expensive seats have already been taken and only the dress circle remains. We have to pay dear to get in."

Dom Eugene expanded on this idea in the foreword he wrote to an edition of Monsignor Escrivá's book *The Way*. "The immediate importance of this book," he said, "is the fact that it is concerned with the inspiring of laymen in the pursuit of perfection. It is hard to single out any need of the present time more important than the development and deepening of the spiritual life of all Catholics, especially that of laymen. Not only is it urgent that the laity be shown that the spiritual life in all its fullness is open to them, but it is also of capital importance that their ordinary work, their professional and social activities, be integrated into their spiritual life and animated by it."

I was happy to have found my way into Opus Dei, where lay people are reminded that God's call to perfection is universal and that this perfection can be achieved in ordinary work and social circumstances. It had also deepened my conviction that teachers are very important to society on account of the influence they exert on their students not only by what they teach, but by what they are.

"The evening lectures on the philosophy of education are fantastic," I told Margaret over coffee. "We have Father O'Cathain, a Jesuit priest, and he's so challenging. He's a disciplinarian and a real teacher. Although the lecture hall is filled with students, I always have the feeling that he's talking to me personally, and the others say they feel the same."

"Somehow good teachers have an influence on your whole life, don't they?" observed Margaret. I heartily agreed.

Father O'Cathain reminded me of Mother St. George, one of my teachers at St. Paul's Academy in Montreal, and my mind slipped back to my childhood.

We moved from Lachine in outer Montreal to Westmount when I was fourteen. By the time I started school there, the semester had already begun, so I was the only newcomer. Dressed in my navy jumper and white blouse, I shyly joined the boisterous girls in the corridor and followed my group to a classroom on the right, where a petite nun in impeccable black habit and distinctive Gothic wimple stood waiting by the open door. She was still and as straight as an arrow, with thin, narrow lips and penetrating gray eyes that seemed to will you to behave well. Only her flushed cheeks betrayed her emotions. There was immediate silence as each one adjusted her books and quietly entered the room, saying, "Good morning, Mother." It was clear that my new teacher was a disciplinarian.

I relished Mother St. George's classes from that first day, when, once we were all seated, she stepped lightly up to the podium and firmly rapped out instructions with an unmistakably British accent which riveted my attention. She taught me for less than a year, but I learned more from her than from all my other teachers put together. She could be quite fiery, but was very just, and I found the high standard of work she exacted challenging. She taught English Literature and Latin, and I loved both. She made sure we understood every expression, every turn of phrase. It was in-depth learning and my first introduction to real study.

All the nuns at that school were very kind, though some were better teachers than others. The geometry teacher was an elderly nun, very pale and gaunt. She made me enjoy geometry—the only area of math in which I have ever done well. She herself was enthusiastic about it, so much so that one freezing winter's day she followed the class out at recess time to continue her lesson, drawing the diagram in the snow with a stick. Like a peripatetic Pythagoras working from diagrams in the sand, she explained the theorem, and we all stood around her, listening. I realized then how contagious a teacher's love for her subject can be . . .

An integral part of the graduate program was student teaching. I was assigned to teach French and English at a girls' school in Blackrock. The children were mostly from Irish-speaking backgrounds, so I had my work cut out for me. This is what I wrote to Mother about my first teaching experiences:

I realized the other evening when Father O'Cathain was speaking that I have been much too engrossed in trying to stick onto my pupils my own ideas and interests. I felt it was enough to walk into the class with my head full of my own ideas on a poem or prose work, and then to pour it into them, as if their minds were simply vessels into which you could pour whatever you liked and have it remain there. But as Father O'Cathain pointed out, that isn't teaching. The most important thing is for the teacher to know her pupils—only then can she hope to arouse their interest, because she will know what interests them. All this sounds self-evident, but it's amazing how long it takes to sink in.

It takes a long time to get over the first self-conscious period, in which one feels awkward and inadequate in the new position of authority. But it's exactly like everything else in life—it's only when you forget yourself and love your class that you are able to do anything with them. At any rate, this morning, instead of selecting an admirable piece of prose and launching into it with them, I selected an account of the Battle of Cuchulain (since the students are all Irish-speaking), and before reading it I asked one of them to tell me the story of Cuchulain.

They were delighted, and all attentive—though not exactly quiet, as they kept interrupting and leaping up to make additions to what was being said. But that was more than desirable! For the weekend composition I've asked them each to write me, in their own words, the legend of Ireland they like best, and they are quite enthusiastic.

I won't go so far as to say the class is a *model* yet, but I feel there is more contact between teacher and pupils, and considerably more good will on both sides. The children instinctively feel when the teacher distrusts or dislikes them and react accordingly. You'd be surprised how easy it is to fall, with the best will in the world, into the temptation of regarding restiveness and giggling by the class as a personal affront. Before you know it you find yourself suspicious and wary of the "little horrors"! You have to take an awful lot with a grain of salt, and forget yourself enough to be able to be *understanding* of them and invulnerable.

At the end of the academic year I took my examination at University College and was awarded a graduate degree in education.

I then moved to Northbrook Residence, bringing with me everything I had. The new piano was a great success. "Wait till Olive comes back from Rome next year—she won't believe her eyes!" exclaimed Beatriz.

This was Olive Mulcahy, who with Teddy was studying at the Roman College of Our Lady. From there they sent us frequent news of "the Father." Anna explained to me that the first people who came into contact with the founder of Opus Dei in the 1930s and benefited from his priestly work had called him simply "the Father." Now his spiritual children and many other people continued to do the same.

One morning Carmen told me, "We're going shopping.

I want to get material to make you a skirt." I was touched. I had left everything when I came to the Work, and never expected to find such concern for my material needs. We went to several shops in search of the right fabric, which turned out to be a soft light wool in a bright blue, gray, and black plaid with a red line running through it. Carmen then suggested getting a black top to go with it, so we bought a woolen one with a collar.

Carmen made for me a lovely pleated skirt. I wore it happily because it was beautiful and because she had made it. During the fittings I learned more about her. She was from Tarrasa, a town near Barcelona which was famous for its fabrics. She had spent her childhood there during the Spanish Civil War. "It was a terrible time," she told me. "Especially the hunger. I was constantly hungry. I remember with anguish a day when one of the Scripture readings at Mass was about the 'land flowing with milk and honey.' I hung on those words and couldn't get that picture out of my mind."

As Carmen talked and worked on my skirt, I thought about how much she and all the others meant to me, and realized that I had found another family that really cared about me—not just about my spiritual well-being, but about everything that concerned me.

In the evenings, after dinner, everyone sat together in the living room for a while, talking companionably about different things. Sometimes Anna came with a letter from Rome, from Encarnita Ortega, and read it out to us.

"Encarnita was one of the first women to join Opus Dei," she explained to me. "That was in 1941. Now she lives in Rome and works with the Father. She and other women from different countries form the Central Advisory, which assists the Father in his work of government."

The letters always brought news of the Father, of his concerns and journeys, and of the development of the Work in various countries of Europe and the Americas.

They were family letters, full of homey details. One evening Anna came with a letter in one hand and a world map in the other.

"Help me find Mozambique, in Africa," she said, spreading the map out on the table. "Encarnita says that the Father has been asked to send people to start the Work there, but that before he can do that we need to be many more." We pored over the map until we located Mozambique, and then read the names of other countries on that vast unfamiliar continent. From my little corner in Northbrook I could scarcely picture the Work in Africa. It seemed so exotic and far away.

The only black people I had ever known were "Bubbie" and "Weeshie." Bubbie came to work for my parents while we were living in D.C., and she became part of the family, staying with us till we moved to Canada. Her real name was Birdie Ford. Part black and part American Indian, she was a small, slight, serious woman with a big nose—which may account for her name. She had great dignity and was a down-to-earth person who spoke her mind and showed her affection by doing rather than saying things. We came to love dearly both her and her daughter, Louisa. Whenever Grannie went out, Birdie made a point of giving her room a thorough cleaning, and Grannie always returned to it exclaiming delightedly, "Birdie, you're an angel!"

Birdie came every day, and several times a week Louisa came along to help with the laundry. Laundry days were very exciting. In the basement there were big sinks, corrugated wooden scrubbing boards, and a big aluminum electric washing machine with a winged hub which moved back and forth, swishing the clothes in soapy water. There was also a large electric mangle that squeezed out the water as the clothes were fed in. Afterwards they were hung on the clotheslines in the backyard. Then Louisa did the ironing, amidst a lovely smell of steam and fresh garments. When my sister Sheila was little she had trouble with her pronunciation, and so she called Birdie "Bubbie" and Louisa "Weeshie," and the names stuck.

When we were allowed to stay home from school with some minor ailment, usually there was nothing wrong with our appetites, so, leaning over the banisters outside our third-floor bedrooms, we would call out, "Bubbie, we're hungry!" And Bubbie would retort, "Sick folks don' eat much!"—and afterwards bring us a generous supply of food.

Our playroom regularly became a mess of papers and toys that one had to wade through. Sometimes Mother came in and scolded us, saying, "Girls, your room is a pigsty!" At other times Bubbie came and helped us tidy up. Once she told us how lucky we were to have such beautiful dolls and toys. When she was a child, she had to make her own doll, with a stick, a potato, and a rag. She cut eyes and a mouth on the potato, and carried it around with her. Brigid and I were deeply moved.

I would have liked to have a black friend at school, but there were no blacks there. At that time everything in D.C. was strictly segregated.

One day when I was about five, I came in after playing outside with friends, and I said the word "nigger." I didn't know what it meant, and certainly didn't direct it at anyone, but Bubbie was there and Mother descended on me like a fury. I was soundly spanked and told to "never, never, never use that word again!" I didn't.

When we were asked what we wanted to be when we grew up, I said, "I want to get married and have ten children," but Brigid said, "I want to be a maid, so everyone will love me." That's how much Bubbie and Weeshie meant to us.

———

The month of May brought a surprise to Northbrook. Anna announced, "A telegram has just arrived saying that Encarnita is coming to Dublin for a few days!" and for once everyone was speechless. Then questions rained down on her—"When is she coming?" "Who will meet her at the airport?" "How long will she stay?"—until she covered her ears with her hands and exclaimed, "I've told you all I know!"

A few days later, at a get-together in the living room of Northbrook, I met Encarnita. A slight woman with dark-blond hair drawn back in a bun, she had strong features and big, lustrous gray eyes that exuded peace and serenity. During the get-together she looked from one to another of us, full of affection. She spoke in Spanish, in a surprisingly deep and resonant voice. With my background in French I could understand most of what she said.

Her presence seemed to bring the Father to us in a very vivid way. She conveyed in a tone of urgency how much the Father was relying on each of us. She also told us about Teddy and Olive, how they were doing at the Roman College of Our Lady, and how vital that institution was to the unity and expansion of the Work. At the Roman College one had the chance to learn the spirit of the Work from the founder himself. It was a great privilege to go there.

My center of gravity shifted from Dublin to Rome, where so much seemed to be happening. I looked with awe at Encarnita, who had been so long in Opus Dei and was working so closely with the Father. Everything she said or did reflected the Father and his teaching, and I thought how much I had to learn from her.

As if guessing my thoughts, she turned to me and said with a smile, "I brought you something from the Father." Then she took from her purse a rosary and a little Italian donkey and put them in my hands, saying, "The Father blessed the rosary for you." I looked at them reverently. I knew how much the Father liked donkeys, and why—because they work so hard, are content with so little, and never kick a master who loves them. He used to refer to himself as a "mangy donkey" and at times comment that "a donkey was Jesus' throne in Jerusalem." I treasured those gifts, my first direct contacts with the Father.

"Would you like to come for a walk with me?" Encarnita asked when the get-together was over. I felt a bit shy, but she soon set me at ease, asking about my family and friends. As we strolled together along Northbrook Road, she asked, "When will you finish your studies at the university?" "I expect to get my degree in June of next year," I told her. Then she asked, "How would you like to come to the Roman College after that?"

I stopped still. Rome, the Pope, the Father . . . it was unbelievable! I would be near the Father and study with women of Opus Dei from many other countries . . .

"I would like it very much," I stammered.

"Then we'll be expecting you," Encarnita said with a smile.

* 4 *

The Roman College

In October 1957 I traveled to Rome with Kathleen Purcell, an Irish girl who had joined Opus Dei in London. A taxi left us at the door of 36 Via di Villa Sacchetti. "To think we're in Rome!" exclaimed Kathleen as we looked around us. To our left, huge scaffoldings with green netting extended all along the road and then around the corner to Bruno Buozzi Avenue. The buildings we had been praying and working for were still under construction, but the Father couldn't wait and have everything ready before bringing his children to the heart of the Work to "Romanize" them.

We were welcomed in the foyer by other students who had arrived before us and already knew their way around the buildings of Villa Sacchetti and La Montagnola which would be our home for the next eight months.

Ours was only the fourth group to come to the Roman College, and there were thirty-two of us from fourteen countries: Germany, Argentina, Colombia, Chile, Ecuador, Spain, the United States, England, Ireland, Italy, Mexico, Peru, Portugal, and Venezuela.

The first outing Kathleen and I made was to St. Peter's Basilica. We said the Creed in front of Saint Peter's tomb, as the Father wanted all his children to do upon arriving in Rome. "Catholic, apostolic, Roman! I want you to be very Roman, ever anxious to make your 'pilgrimage' to Rome *videre Petrum*—to see Peter" (*The Way*, no. 520).

The houses were not equipped for so many people. We overflowed everywhere, using makeshift beds, sharing closets, lining up for showers, carrying our chairs from place to place, well aware of the privilege it was to be there at all. We lived with the directors of the Central Advisory. One of them, Lourdes Toranzo, from the Canary Islands, was the director of the course we would be taking.

She went over the daily schedule with us, which included cleaning first thing in the morning and working on the furnishing and decorating of the house. There was a program of classes given by women and by priests of Opus Dei, and time for study.

"When will we see the Father?" we all eagerly asked. "Probably on the opening day of the course," replied Lourdes.

The course officially began on October 24, feast of Saint Raphael, and that was the day I saw Monsignor Escrivá for the first time. "The Father is coming this evening," Encarnita told us, and everyone cheered. "Be sure to be ready and waiting in the living room in good time."

I hurried along the corridor of the Madonna, my heart thumping. What would it be like to meet the Father? How would he know who I was? What would I say? Those in front of me had already turned right and gone into La Montagnola and were climbing the cream-colored marble staircase with brass banister which led to the living room on the second floor. Lourdes was waiting for us and showed us how to arrange the furniture in the room, leaving at the far end a seat for the Father and another for Don Alvaro, who always accompanied him. The other chairs and a matching stool were placed in front at a discreet distance and the large woolen rugs cleared for sitting on.

"Make sure everyone has a place to sit," Lourdes cautioned. "The Father wouldn't like to find anyone sitting on the cold tiles."

As it was already dusk, the lights were on and the shutters half closed. The room was full of people and our voices rose in excited chatter. Every now and then

Encarnita and Lourdes, who were standing by the door, turned to smile at us and occasionally laid a finger on their lips, and the noise died down for a while.

Suddenly I heard the loud click of the metal handle of the sanctuary door on the floor beneath and the sound of voices and rapid footsteps approaching the staircase. As Encarnita and Lourdes went forward to meet the Father, I heard a rich, vibrant voice that was unmistakably his. I was standing in the front, near the door, and as the footsteps drew nearer I strained to catch my first glimpse of the Father. Soon he was at the door, with Don Alvaro behind him. The Father paused briefly on the threshold and looked around warmly at us all from behind dark-rimmed glasses, a smile playing about his lips. He was wearing a plain black cassock with white clerical collar. His face was pale, and he had full cheeks and a broad forehead with deep grooves. His dark hair was parted and combed to one side.

"Pax, my daughters," he said, as he moved purposefully to the seat reserved for him. "In aeternum!" we replied in unison. We had learned from him this greeting—a greeting of peace, evangelical and eternal, followed by a heartfelt response that the peace might be truly eternal.

After asking how we were, the Father spoke about the purpose of our stay in Rome. He explained that at the Roman College of Our Lady, many hearts come together to form a single heart beating with the same love; many wills unite with the one desire of serving God; and intellects come together, open to receive all the truths which enlighten our common divine vocation. It is called Roman, he said, because in our soul and spirit we are very Roman and because the Holy Father, the Vicar of Christ, lives in Rome. And the "of our Lady" is because we also place ourselves under the mantle of our Lady, Mother of God and our Mother, under whose protection we are safe.

He deeply loved the Roman College and told us what hopes he had for it. With time, he said, women from every nation of the world would go there and later be a powerful force for unity in their different countries. There was an urgent need to spread the teachings of Christ; we should store up our training, fill ourselves with clear ideas, with the fullness of the Christian message, and then pass it on to others. He told us he needed the support of our loyalty and fidelity to our way, and urged us to fulfill well the norms of the plan of life. "The specific norms your director gave you and explained to you, and made you love: be faithful to them and you will be an apostle."

Before he left we knelt down to receive his blessing, and on his way out he raised both hands and said, "May God bless you!"

With this blessing the academic year of our Roman College started.

Our day began with the cleaning of the house. On the first morning I didn't know what to do, as everything seemed to me so clean already. I stood in the corridor, in my white smock, watching the others scurry right and left with mops and buckets. I got a duster and started wiping the table in the first bedroom, wondering how I would fill the whole half hour. Then another student, a doctor from Mexico named Obdulia Rodríguez, came and took me in hand. She gave me a practical lesson on cleaning marble floors and applying "overlay," on mopping the bedroom tiles, and on the art of using a feather duster. After that the cleaning became a vigorous exercise; the half hours flew by and at the end I was perspiring like the rest.

All the upholstering and decorating was done at home. The Father had limitless confidence in the ability of his daughters and encouraged us all to make use of our talents—"everyone who wants to . . . the more the better, even if it's only with a brushstroke!" He wanted ours to be comfortable, but not luxurious, Christian homes. So we had to create them ourselves, with our ingenuity, and he himself showed us how to do this as cheaply but as attractively as possible, since, as he put it, poverty doesn't mean neglect.

"Mercedes is making a new set of altar linens as a surprise for the Father's birthday," Lourdes announced one afternoon from the door of the living room, where some of us were studying. "It will make him happy to know that everyone helped, so anyone who likes is invited to put in at least one stitch." I put down my Church history notes and hurried to the sewing room, where I found Mercedes Angles, a professional seamstress, surrounded by students and hovering anxiously over them, one by one. Some sewed well and were allowed to put in as many stitches as they liked. When my turn came, she held her breath as I awkwardly took up the needle, pierced the material with it, and drew the thread through. She couldn't take it away fast enough. But I was happy to have contributed my stitch.

Helena Serrano had an artistic flair, and the Father wanted to give it free rein. As soon as a suitable blank wall became available he told her, "It's all yours! There's a wide space for you to paint to your heart's content. Why don't you make a big map of the world, showing where there are centers of the women of the Work? There are already so many around the globe."

Clustered around the marble-topped coffee table, seated on the available chairs or on the rug, we "visited" one country after another as each one told stories about the apostolic work going on in her region. We also discovered one another's talents. Everyone was ready to do anything to give the others a good time. No one ever said she couldn't or she didn't know how.

The most thrilling sound in the house was when the intercom rang out on every floor with the message, "Tell everyone to go straight to the living room—the Father is coming! Make sure you don't leave anyone out." A quick touch-up before the mirror, a change of shoes . . . and I was hurrying along the corridor with the rest.

The Father had a deep personal affection for his children. Once he told Catherine Bardinet, "Yesterday I saw you from a distance on the street, and I prayed to your guardian angel for you, as I always do when I see one of you." It wasn't surprising, then, that we responded with our love.

This time I found a place on the rug beside the coffee table just in front of the Father. On the table there was a collection of tiny Murano glass ducks in different colors, and every now and then the Father picked one up and toyed with it. His hands were very white, with pronounced veins and long, expressive fingers. I knew the meaning of the little ducks. The Father liked ducks because when they're thrown into the water they immediately start swimming. Some have wide-open beaks; these are frank and speak up. Others have theirs shut tight; they know how to keep quiet and never gossip.

"Ducks, to water!" he would tell us. "If I ask anything of you, my daughters, never say it's impossible—I know that already. Since I began the Work, our Lord has asked of me many things that were impossible, but that nevertheless worked out. That's why I want you to be like ducks that dive into the water without hesitation or fear. If God asks for something, one must do it, one must swim—straight ahead, courageously. Now do you understand why I love these creatures so much?" We understood from this that the Father could ask us to go anywhere at any time. I was eager that he be able to trust me and send me out to swim, like a duck, in strange waters. I was filled with the enthusiasm and eagerness of youth, and dreamed of distant and exotic places where there was work to be done.

The Father spoke energetically and with urgency, yet never seemed to be in a hurry. His rich, warm voice conveyed simplicity and great sincerity. Every now and then he would stop and, looking around at us all, ask, "What have you to tell me, my daughters?" and we would willingly tell him.

Joan McIntosh, from the United States, once asked, "Father, why do we speak of our life in the Work as 'family life'?"

The Father smiled at her. "Being the good teacher you are," he said, "you could explain that perfectly well to the others . . . but you want to hear it from me, don't you? You know that we speak of 'family life' because our houses have the same atmosphere as that of other Christian families. Our houses are not schools, nor barracks; they are homes where people of the same family live together. God himself is our Father, and the Mother of God is our Mother. Moreover, we have a real affection for one another."

Then he leaned forward and, knitting his fingers, pressed his hands together in an eloquent gesture that reinforced his words. "We really love one another," he said. "I don't want anyone in the Work to ever feel alone!"

The Father then told us the Roman College would one day have its own premises, with sports facilities and ample living accommodations, "but you have more grace." I was very grateful to God to have come when I did. The greatest grace was to live near the founder and receive the spirit of the Work from his own lips.

He spoke to us dynamically about the expansion of the Work to other countries, saying that an immense work awaited us which should be a stimulus for our struggle to be faithful to the commitment we had made.

Then he paused, looked down at me, and with a penetrating look, full of affection, asked, "Are you going to be faithful, my daughter?" I replied with all my heart, "Yes, Father!"

Nisa Guzman was living in Rome at that time. She was

one of the first women of Opus Dei; she had joined in 1941, with Encarnita. In Spain she had been an extraordinary woman for her time, having studied several languages and traveled widely. In 1950 she had gone to Chicago to work there and introduce the spirit of Opus Dei to women in the United States. Now she was preparing to do the same in Montreal. She told me, laughing, "I'm a cold-natured person—I hope I don't freeze!"

Since my family was living in Montreal, Nisa often talked to me about Canada and I wrote to tell my parents about her. Not long afterwards, she and Laura Poblete went to Montreal to start a center there. My parents let them stay with them until their own house was ready. Mother wrote that she felt privileged to be asked to keep the priest's vestments in one of her closets until the oratory was finished. Nisa, knowing Mother was an artist, also asked her to paint an altarpiece. In the art gallery they chose a Madonna for Mother to reproduce.

The expansion the Father had spoken about was becoming a reality that affected us personally. Laura had left for Canada, Catherine was making trips to France (her native land), and Lourdes told us often that we should be prepared for anything the Work might need of us.

That advice took on a new dimension the day she came with this exciting news: "Opus Dei is going to start up on two new continents—in Japan and in Kenya! There are people of the Work here who have visited those countries, and the Father has asked them to give you a couple of talks."

The first talk was on Japan. "It is a country with an ancient culture and a strong work ethic," the speaker said. "Both the language and the style of living are very different from those of the West. It is a whole new world, with great possibilities at the university."

That talk gave rise to lots of speculation. "Who do you

think will go?" "I hear that Japanese is very hard to learn." "Don Alvaro studied it during the Spanish Civil War, remember?" "It's so far . . . but imagine how exciting!"

Then we had a talk on Kenya, where Opus Dei was soon to start its work on the African continent. "Christianity is still new to Kenya, just over sixty years old, so it's like living in the times of the early Christians." We glanced furtively at one another, arrested by fleeting images of the catacombs and of Christians thrown to the lions.

"In the missions," the speaker went on, unawares, "the faithful are called to Mass by the beating of a drum." I imagined a drum hanging from a tree like a gong, and a man beating it with a stick. "As yet Kenya doesn't have a university and women get little, if any, formal education. There is a great task ahead for the women who go to start the Work there." I wondered if I might be one of those women. For the remainder of my time in Rome I dreamt of those two faraway countries.

The months flew by, and soon the shuttered windows were flung open to let in the light and warmth of a Roman spring. There seemed to be a renewed zest for everything, and I felt secure—at home with my jobs, coping with the language and studies, and at one with the others, especially the Father. Each new day was a bonus to be treasured, because the course was coming to an end. I had mixed feelings. It would be hard to leave Rome, the Father, all the others who would be returning to their countries . . . and yet there was so much to be done.

A day came when Encarnita called me. "How would you like to return to Dublin tomorrow?" she asked with a smile. All my castles in the air evaporated and with a thud I came down to reality.

"I'd be glad to," I answered, truthfully.

Travel arrangements were made, and all that remained

was to receive the Father's blessing. I looked forward to that moment eagerly, with a mixture of sadness and joy. I knew that in the Work we never say good-bye, since, as the Father often reminded us, we are always spiritually united. Nevertheless, parting was painful.

"Be ready in the corridor *degli Uccelli* [of the birds]," Encarnita advised the four of us who were leaving the following day, "in case the Father can receive you after dinner." We arrived well ahead of time and paced up and down the brown marble floor together, rosaries in hand, under the bright ceiling full of colorful painted birds from which the corridor got its name.

Then the door to the service area opened. "Hurry, Encarnita is waiting for you!" We hastened along to the narrow staircase that led up to the dining room of Villa Tevere. Encarnita met us at the foot of the stairs, and we climbed up to the landing single file. There she opened the door, and we entered to find the Father waiting for us at the end of a large mahogany table surrounded by red velvet chairs. Don Alvaro was beside him.

"Sit down, sit down," the Father told us, and we sat around the table, with the Father at the head. He looked slowly from one to the other with fatherly affection, and then gave Lolita Iñíguez a big china duck for Eigelstein, our residence in Cologne, and told Encarnita to make sure we all had something to bring home with us.

Then he asked Don Alvaro if the pictures of our Lady that had just come off the printing press at Villa Sacchetti were dry. Don Alvaro nodded and produced five. The Father then wrote on the back of each, "Cor Mariae Dulcissimum, iter para tutum! [Most Sweet Heart of Mary, prepare a safe way!] Roma, 28–V–58," and handed them to us as he finished, one by one. He suggested that whenever we said that prayer we also ask for fidelity to the way to which our Lord had called us.

After we knelt down and received his blessing, the Father turned on his heels and rapidly left the room. I realized then that it was hard for him to see his children go, and my heart went out to him. Never did I suspect how soon I would be seeing him again.

Plenty of work awaited me in Dublin. I was appointed assistant director of Northbrook Residence, which is a corporate undertaking of Opus Dei, meaning that Opus Dei is answerable for the doctrinal and spiritual guidance given there. The governing body of the center consisted of Pilarín Lázaro (the director), María Teresa Valdés (the secretary), and me.

"Government in the Work is always collegial," I had been taught in Rome, "involving at least three persons, like a stool resting on three legs. If one of the legs is missing, the stool can't stand upright." I was the one most directly responsible for the running of the residence and its activities.

A chaplain celebrated daily Mass and came to look after the spiritual needs of both staff and students.

In the following year, on Tuesday, August 18, the Father came to Ireland—the only visit he ever made to this land, which he dearly loved. With Don Alvaro del Portillo and Don Javier Echevarría, he visited us in the living room of Northbrook, where three chairs had been placed in front of the marble chimneypiece's ornate mirror and the rest of the furniture had been arranged so that everyone had room to sit either on it or on the carpet. I felt as if I were in Rome again.

The Father encouraged us to do a lot of apostolate because many dedicated souls were needed to spread Opus Dei to other countries, such as Kenya, Japan, and Austria. "Ireland has a mission in the world," he said, "especially throughout the English-speaking world, which is half the globe. Many Irish women are needed, here, there, everywhere. Ireland is a marvelous country. It is the consolation of God, with its good, splendid people. . . . I hope to come again next year around this time, but you must multiply tenfold. You have to be cheerful, eager to go out all over the world to serve God, for love of Jesus Christ."

The Father had a passion for souls, and he instilled this in us. "In Dublin, in Rome, in Madrid, just as in the middle of Africa, souls! That's what matters! If you love the Lord, you will necessarily become aware of the blessed burden of souls that need to be brought to God." It impressed me to hear him saying in Dublin the same things he had so often told us in Rome.

At the beginning of that academic year a West African student from Gambia applied for admission to Northbrook Residence. I was in charge of admissions and wondered what to do, as we had never had an African resident before and I had no idea how she would fit in. I consulted Pilarín and María Teresa, and Pilarín said without hesitation, "Of course she should come! The Father has always insisted that our centers are open to everyone." And so Harriet Joof came to live at Northbrook.

Harriet was a simple, straightforward person with a big heart and a good sense of humor, and she made friends with everybody. Tall and slim, she usually was bundled up in coveralls and thick cardigans and kept her head wrapped up in a scarf, as the cold, damp weather was very trying for her. I soon caught on that the scarf was like a thermometer. The lower her spirits, the further down the rolled scarf would be, sometimes nearly covering her eyes. When she was in good spirits, it rested jauntily on the top of her head. She showed us with nostalgia photos of her family homestead in West Africa, which was set in a bright, sunny clearing with thatched clay huts surrounded by palm trees.

In December Father José María Hernández de Garnica visited Northbrook again. I hadn't seen him since that memorable day of October 24, 1955, when he celebrated Mass in its oratory. This time he came on a bicycle, his cassock wound around his waist. Much to my surprise, he entered through the kitchen door, while

Maire and I were preparing dinner. "Call the others," he said. "We can meet here in the dining room."

I ran upstairs with the news that Father José María was waiting, and in a jiffy they were all there. We pulled the chairs around in a circle and everyone sat down.

"How are you getting on?" he asked. Pilarín told him, among other things, about the resident from West Africa.

"You know, the men are already established in Kenya and in Japan," he said. "It's time for the women to go there. We need English-speaking people, and Kenya needs teachers." He looked around at us all with a puckish smile and added, "Any volunteers?" Everyone, including me, answered, "Yes!"

5

Preparing for Africa

"Pilarín would like to see you as soon as possible," Olive announced one evening in March 1960, while I was drying the dishes after dinner.

I sensed something out of the ordinary in the wind as I entered Pilarín's office. She was waiting for me with an air of suppressed excitement. "Come in and sit down," she said kindly, rising from behind her desk and moving towards the two easy chairs in front of the door. We sat down, and then she said, "You know, the Father wants the women of Opus Dei to start the Work in Kenya and Japan very soon . . ."

I thought I could guess what was coming. Would it be Kenya or Japan?

"The Father wants to know if you would like to go to Kenya."

My heart stopped. I realized that something very big was going to happen, and its magnitude was earth-shattering to me. To dream about starting on a new continent was one thing; to actually go there was quite another. Kenya seemed strange and very far away. But what an adventure! The Father had such great hopes for the expansion of the Work to Africa, and he was asking me. Could I do it? I was so young and inexperienced. What did I know about Africa? Not even where Kenya was on the map! My heart beat fast. But if the Father asked me, it was because he thought I could do it . . . so I surely would. Pilarín was looking at me steadily while these thoughts ran through my mind.

"You don't have to answer right away," she said. "The Father wants you to think about it slowly and then write and give him your answer perfectly freely."

Shaking off any misgivings, I said firmly, "I do want to go. I'll write to the Father tonight."

Now the die was cast. I had no doubt that I wanted to go, but I already sensed the pain there would be in leaving behind everything familiar. Once again I was facing a departure, but this time it was I who would be leaving my Northbrook family behind.

Not long afterwards Pilarín told me that I had been appointed to Kenya and María Teresa to Japan. That meant two of us from Northbrook. The following morning at breakfast I looked across the table at María Teresa, and suddenly it struck me how Japanese she looked, with her round face, slanted eyes, and curved, delicate hands.

Pilarín brought more news. Two others would be going from London: Kathleen to Japan, and Margaret Curran to Kenya. And then, looking at me with great affection and understanding, anticipating my reaction, she exclaimed, "The Father wants you all to go to Rome for a workshop before going on to your new countries!"

This wonderful news filled me with a sense of relief and real security. Here I was feeling torn about leaving my family, but the Father, in his loving care, was calling us to the larger family in Rome, to be strengthened and renewed, to have our knowledge of the spirit of the Work deepened, and to get preparation for the work of expansion before journeying into the unknown.

Harriet, overjoyed that I was going to Africa, took me in hand and told me all she could. Together we pored over her photos of her village.

"Everything is done in the open air," she explained. "The women prepare the food and cook it on stones outside the huts, and then it is eaten under the palm trees. We only use the huts for sleeping. The women do all the chores. They fetch water, gather firewood, cook, plant, harvest, go to the market, mind the children . . ."

"What about the men?" I asked.

"They sit together and drink and talk. They make all the decisions and are very respected. Most of the men have several wives. Each wife has her own hut in the husband's compound where she stays with her children."

That sounded very strange to me. "Don't they quarrel?" I asked.

"Not really," answered Harriet. "It's an accepted thing that if a man prospers he can afford more wives. He needs them to till his land and they give him more children."

"It seems like women are treated like possessions," I said incredulously.

"That's true," Harriet said, "they are. Daughters mean wealth because they bring a dowry into the home, so usually they are married off at an early age, while boys are given as much education as possible, especially the eldest son, who will then help educate the younger ones. These are the country's future chiefs or leaders. Fathers don't think of educating girls since they will go off to another family anyway; a woman always passes to the clan of her husband. There she must carry out the traditional chores and bear children."

"Does every woman have to get married?" I asked.

"She has no choice. First she belongs to her father and then to her husband. It is unthinkable for a girl to remain single."

"But Harriet, you're here getting an education. Surely there must be other girls who are educated like you?"

"Very few, although with Christianity things are beginning to change. My father is an exceptional man. He realizes the importance of education and encouraged me to complete my schooling and go on to a university in Europe. Education is the only hope for women in Africa to break free from their subservient condition, but most of them don't even realize it."

"Oh, Harriet," I exclaimed, "I'm so glad that I'm going to teach there!" I believed in the power of education to change lives. I was eager for this chance to make a difference in an area of such vital importance as the education of women in Africa.

I visited people I thought could assist me, among them Mr. Digby, a friend of Therese's family and a prominent businessman. I visited him at his office and explained to him my plans for going to Kenya. He listened attentively and then said, "Let me help you with the plane ticket," and promptly made out a check. As he handed it to me, he added, "When you get to Nairobi, look up a friend of mine, John Hughes, and tell him I sent you. He will be able to help you there." As it turned out, I had reason to be very grateful for that introduction.

But Mr. John Hughes was not the first contact I had for Nairobi. Mrs. Agnes Lavelle was waiting impatiently for the women of Opus Dei to come to Kenya. She had been corresponding for months with Teddy, and those blue air letters with the Kenyan stamps and the drawings of wild animals on them had attracted my attention.

"The priests of Opus Dei hold monthly days of recollection for women in Nairobi," Teddy had told us. "Mrs. Lavelle says they take place in the chapel of a girls' school and about a dozen ladies attend."

Teddy wrote to tell Mrs. Lavelle that I was going to Africa, and she got back an enthusiastic letter full of useful information. "Tell Olga not to bring a raincoat," wrote Mrs. Lavelle, "because she won't need it. Either it doesn't rain at all or it rains so heavily that a raincoat is useless."

As the day of departure approached, my heart grew heavy at the thought of leaving so much that was dear and familiar behind, perhaps forever. I had grown up in Ireland. I had studied and made friends there. I loved the country and its people, and it was in Ireland that I had discovered the reason for my existence. Life at Northbrook was going on as usual, but soon I would no longer be part of it.

In the midst of the excitement of packing, it hit me forcefully one evening that I was really going away into the unknown. As the others trooped noisily upstairs after dinner, I stayed behind and cast a nostalgic look around the familiar dining room, scene of so many happy memories. Suddenly overwhelmed, I pressed my face against the old wooden dining room door and burst into tears. But soon it passed and I was ready to go.

Kathleen had come to Ireland to say good-bye to her family, and we embarked together on the night mail boat departing from Dun Laoghaire Harbor. After a last hearty embrace, Pilarín, Beatriz, and Olive left us and stood waving on the quay as the boat steamed out of the harbor.

We watched as the shoreline rapidly receded. It was already dark, but I could make out the shapes of the houses above the rocky coves, their lights gleaming from afar. Suddenly there appeared the house where I had lived with my family before they went to Canada.

"Look," I cried, pointing to the shore, "there's Beulah!"

"Where? What's that?" asked Kathleen.

"It's the house in Dalkey where I lived with my family for five years. From my bedroom window I often watched the mail boat come and go . . ."

"Beulah" was a pale blue, rambling, rather shabbily furnished house that had two pillars at the entrance and a long curved driveway sweeping between overgrown gardens that stretched right down to the seafront. Inside, it had several gracious reception rooms with bay windows, and one wide hall with a spacious dressing room.

The house had been perfect for parties. In my second year at Trinity College Mother gave me an eighteenth-birthday party—a ball, complete with orchestra. She went to a lot of trouble over it. The driveway was hung with lighted Chinese lanterns, the ground-floor rooms were flung open to make a large dance hall, and the orchestra played away. Each girl was given a ball book with an original drawing by Mother on the front, a pencil hanging from a ribbon, and the list of dances inside, with blanks for the young men to fill in. The gentlemen came in dinner jackets, and the ladies in long dresses. My parents opened the dance with a waltz, and I was very proud of them as they whirled around the room in perfect unison, Daddy's coattails flying. The party was a great success, and my friends still remind me of it.

Beulah was an open house for all our friends. "Mrs. Marlin, how many people for lunch?" the cook—stout, apple-cheeked Peggy from County Wexford—would ask, hands on hips. "Your guess is as good as mine, Peggy," my mother would answer with a resigned sigh.

My college friends were regular visitors, and my sister and best friend Brigid, who is a year younger than me and was then a student at the Academy of Art, was very popular with them. While we talked or played music, thirteen-year-old Sheila would bustle in and out, intent on her own affairs and followed by her pals from school. Liz, at eight, had a passion for the age of chivalry and the noble adventures of the Knights of the Round Table which she shared with her best friend, Paschal Greaves. My brothers, Randal and John, came home to Beulah during vacations from their school in England, sometimes bringing along a friend or two. The house resounded with music and laughter, jokes and the occasional quarrel . . .

"It's like waving good-bye to the past, isn't it?" I said, watching the lights on the shore vanish as the boat forged ahead into the open sea.

———

"Parioli, Via di Villa Sacchetti, trentasei, per favore!" I said as Kathleen and I climbed into the cab at Stazioni Termini. We had plenty of luggage, as we had brought not only our own things but also many gifts we had been given for the new centers in Kenya and Japan. The Fiat careened through the traffic, now and then stopping in the nick of time, evidencing the amazing skill of Roman drivers. "Qui! Qui!" I called out as we reached the turn-in to Villa Sacchetti. There stood the long ocher façade—all the scaffolding gone now—with its inset antiqued olive green door. While I rang the bell, Kathleen and I beamed at one another. How wonderful to be back again!

Exclamations and welcoming embraces abounded while ready hands grasped our bags. "Did you have a good journey?" "Yes, we did. How is the Father?" "He's very well, and looking forward to seeing you all." After a brief visit to the Blessed Sacrament, we were accompanied to our rooms.

No sooner had I put down my bags than I was told, "Tere Temes wants to meet you, but she's sick in bed with the flu. Can you come see her?" I had heard of Tere—Father José María Hernández de Garnica's niece, who was also going to Kenya—and I went eagerly.

Tere was sitting up waiting for me, on a bed littered with books and magazines about Kenya. After the first greetings, we took a closer look at each other. Tere and I were to share over thirty years of life in Nairobi. She was very pale and had a high forehead, thick brown hair, and remarkably thick, straight eyebrows; a large aristocratic nose; a generous mouth which often broke into laughter; brown eyes that were full of life and seemed to take in everything. She exuded confidence and was energetic and decisive and never at a loss for words. Now she was smiling and offering to show me what she had found in the magazines. Tere had a degree in history and had lost no time familiarizing herself with the background of our new country. I was very impressed and reassured by our having a person like Tere coming with us to Kenya.

A few days later Mary Mahoney arrived from Boston. She had served in the U.S. Army, where she worked as a nurse, reaching the rank of major, and had come into contact with Opus Dei through her mother, who was a close friend of Nisa Guzman. Curiously, she had only recently returned from service in Japan. Mary struck me as a rather shy but very caring person with a spirit of adventure and wanderlust.

Margaret Curran was a dimpled Irishwoman with short, curly dark hair and brown eyes. She had a volatile temperament and a great sense of humor—which was to lighten many a situation. It would prove providential that Margaret was a secretary by profession.

At twenty, Marlene Sousa, a Portuguese girl who for some years had lived with her family in Angola, was the youngest. A tall girl with dark hair and deep black eyes, she had a lovely, elegant figure and was very pretty. She had an even temper and was very artistic.

Rosario Insausti, Encarnación Riera, and Elisa Serrano, all of whom were qualified in the hospitality profession, were coming with us to work and teach in Kenya. Rosario was simplicity itself—very outgoing, with an inexhaustible spirit of service. Encarnación was a thrifty, hardworking person with a lot of drive—an excellent cook and seamstress. Elisa had a colorful, poetic personality and an instinctive understanding of people and situations. She was also a nervous and sensitive person.

Those three were destined to have a tremendous impact on the concept people had of domestic work. The Father had instilled in them a deep pride in their work of caring for others and creating a home. Like little seeds, they would bring forth an army of Kenyan numerary assistants. These numeraries are absolutely essential to the good running of the centers of the Work, making them truly family homes, and also to the whole apostolate of Opus Dei, because what first attracts people is the atmosphere of the centers, which from there is passed on to the whole of society.

"You can't imagine how involved everyone here has

been in preparing our journeys to Kenya and Japan," Tere told me. "María Luisa's office is piled high with books and teaching materials sent from other countries for the schools in Nairobi and Osaka. The plan is to start with a finishing school in Nairobi where we can teach languages, literature, home economics, crafts, and general knowledge to girls of all races, preparing them for their future roles in society. African women haven't been given the same opportunities for education and social exposure as men."

African men were getting better educated, coming up in the world, and getting exposed to Western culture. The women, on the other hand, tended to remain in the villages, with little or no opportunity to advance, and so were at a loss when it came to attending public functions with their husbands. I realized the importance of women's education, but since Harriet had told me that African women were restricted in their freedom, I could only hope that some would be able to come to our school.

On the first day of the workshop, the Father came to see us at La Montagnola. He told us he was very happy because we were going to start the Work in three new countries (Kenya, Japan, and Austria) with enthusiasm, joy, and an unwavering fidelity.

He insisted on the importance of our identifying with the mentality and customs of our new countries and not hankering after what we had left behind. "When we begin our work in a country," he said, "we cannot isolate ourselves, but must form roots in it. Otherwise nothing will succeed. For it is not our business to represent national interests, but rather to serve Jesus Christ and the Holy Church." This meant adapting to local customs regarding food and clothing, rather than asserting our foreign background.

The Father reminded us that we were going to learn. Our role, he said, was to be like that of the stick placed beside a young tree to help it grow strong and upright, until it can stand on its own. The deepest work would be done by the people we formed in the countries we went to.

He spoke with great affection about the African people. "They have been treated very badly," he said. "They have the right to be treated marvelously well, and the best way to make that happen is to treat them as equals. We are equal! We can't claim the slightest difference." He insisted that all humans are made of the same clay and speak the same language—that of the heart—and have the same color, that of children of the same Father, and that there is really only one race, that of the children of God.

The condition that African women were in was of great concern to the Father. "They are treated like objects to be used!" he lamented. Our job was to help change this through education and by upholding the Christian view of the dignity of women.

On Easter Sunday we were able to attend the Father's Mass, and he told us he was offering it for us. In his homily he urged us to take care of our prayer life, and added firmly, with great conviction, "You are not going alone, because you are going with Christ and we are all with Christ."

The Father was concerned about our families, since we were going so far away, so he asked us to write to them from Rome and send photos. Tere was the eldest of twelve children, the youngest of whom was only three. When she informed her family in Madrid that she was going to Kenya, her twelve-year-old brother wrote back, "Wow, what luck! You're off to the jungle!" The Father was very amused when she told him about it.

Everything seemed to accelerate during our last days in Rome. We needed to be inoculated against cholera and yellow fever, and I welcomed Encarnita's suggestion, "If you like, Catherine could accompany you to the Istituto di Sanità." The diseases sounded horrible and I was apprehensive, especially since Tere had a reaction and her whole arm swelled.

Several blue letters arrived from Agnes Lavelle. She and some friends had found a house for us in Nairobi and were busy getting it ready. "I hope you will like it," she wrote. "It has been rented for one year, and should be big enough for your school."

Meanwhile I was notified that my application for a teaching position with the Ministry of Education had been approved and I was assigned to the Kenya Girls' High School. Margaret would have no problem getting employment as a secretary and Mary as a nurse, though they would have to apply in person. So we would be able to support ourselves.

We were booked on a flight leaving June 12, which in that year, 1960, was Trinity Sunday. In his homily that morning Father José Luis Soria made the most of the day's Gospel reading, the last part of which couldn't have been more appropriate: "Go therefore and make disciples of all nations . . ." (Mt 28:20).

I was torn by conflicting emotions: those connected with, on the one hand, leaving Rome and the Father for who knew how long, my responsibility for the others going with me, the unknowns awaiting us at the other end of the journey . . . and on the other, the confidence the Father placed in us, the adventure of starting work on a new continent, a great desire to live and work among the African people, for whom the Father showed such a clear predilection . . .

But there wasn't time for nursing my emotions. The day was full of last-minute messages and recommendations, and at any moment we might be called for the blessing of the Father.

When that time came, we gathered in the living room of La Montagnola with Encarnita and other members of the Central Advisory. It seemed unreal to me, and I had a knot in my chest. The Father came in with Don Alvaro and asked if we were happy. Then he urged us once again to look after fulfilling the norms of the plan of life, reminding us that everything else was secondary.

He had presents for us. He brought out and blessed two gold medals of Saint Joseph, each on a gold chain with pearls, for the keys to the tabernacles in the first women's centers in Osaka and Nairobi. He gave one to María Teresa and the other to me, and then, turning to Don Alvaro, asked, "What else can we give these daughters?" He looked around at us all with deep affection and I thought he would have given us the moon if he could. After giving us his blessing, he said that he was very proud and happy and that we were going to do a colossal work.

Before leaving the house that night, the eight of us went to pray before the Madonna of the Colonnata, in a small courtyard on the grounds of Villa Sacchetti. I had often gone there to switch on the light—a sign of the protection of our Lady, to remain shining throughout the night. As we prayed the Memorare, I entrusted to her all the people that awaited us in our new country, Kenya.

Encarnita rode with us to Ciampino Airport. She said to Mary Ribero, who was driving, "Take us by St. Peter's so they can have a last look at the Basilica." I was very grateful, and craned my neck to keep the great illuminated dome in view as long as possible. Eventually we reached the airport, where everything was a flurry of tickets, suitcases, and farewells. In no time the British Airways plane en route to Nairobi was ready for boarding.

* 6 *

The Beginning of an Adventure

None of us could sleep that night; we were too excited. I was filled with vivid impressions of our last day in Rome and kept thinking of the Father, who would be accompanying us with his prayer.

The plane landed in Khartoum very early in the morning, when it was still totally dark. "Let's have something to eat," suggested Marlene. "They packed snacks for us in the carry-on luggage." She rummaged around and then exclaimed delightedly, "*Turrones* and whole cheeses!" We each had a piece of Christmas nougat, grateful for the thoughtfulness of those we had left behind.

Soon the jet was speeding forward again. A moment came when a bright orange line appeared all along the horizon. It widened rapidly until the whole sky began to glow, and soon it was iridescent daylight, sparkling so clear and bright that it dazzled my eyes and I had to lower the window shade. That was our first glimpse of the scintillating, incredibly beautiful African daylight.

At last the jet landed at Embakasi Airport. When it came to a halt we took down the carry-on luggage and jostled our way to the narrow exit, where we were met by a wave of hot, dry air. The immense expanse of clear blue sky, with here and there thin wisps of cloud, stretched away on all sides and seemed much higher than in Europe. Around us as far as the eye could see lay dry yellow plains. There was a great stillness, broken only by an occasional shout or the cry of a bird. Mary took a deep breath. "The air feels good here, clean and kind of exhilarating," she said. I was overwhelmed by my responsibility for this little group just arriving to start working on an unfamiliar continent, and eagerly anticipated the welcome of the Father's representative in Kenya, the Counsellor.

As we walked along the tarmac towards the miniature two-story airport, I looked hopefully at the waiting station, but it was empty. "It doesn't look as if anyone has come to meet us," I said to Mary, disappointed. "Maybe they're inside," she replied.

There we found British airport officials wearing open white shirts, short white trousers, and knee-length socks, and barefooted African porters dressed in long white gowns and maroon fezzes. The atmosphere was casual and relaxed. There were no barriers to pass, and once our papers and suitcases had been cleared we were free. But no one had come to meet us. As we stood huddled together, uncertain what to do next, an official came up and pointed out an airport bus that would take us into Nairobi.

While the bus ambled along in the bright morning sunshine, we looked eagerly out the windows, hoping to catch a glimpse of a zebra or a giraffe, but only the dry savanna appeared, stretching to the horizon on both sides.

When we neared the town, Princess Elizabeth Highway divided into two, with one-way traffic on either side of an island stretching all along the way, filled with colorful bougainvillea tables and tall palm trees. Alongside the road we saw flowering trees and occasionally an umbrella-shaped thorn tree with thin, outspread branches. "How beautiful!" exclaimed Marlene. "This town is set in the middle of a garden." We came upon several traffic circles encompassing carefully tended rock gardens filled with cacti and tropical plants.

The bus kept following the outer white line and then turned right and stopped in front of the airport terminal on Hardinge Street. We clambered down, collected our luggage, and found ourselves at the end of a long, dusty road lined with uneven one-story buildings. "It looks like a town in a Wild West movie," Mary whispered. "All that's missing is a hitching post for horses!"

"What are we going to do?" asked Elisa, anxiously.

"I'll try to call Mrs. Lavelle," I said, heading for the terminal door. We entered the dark, cramped little office, and I asked for a phone book. Agnes' number was there, but when I called, no one answered. Then I thought of Mrs. Hearn, a woman from Nairobi whom I had met in Rome. Her name was also in the book, and this time I got an answer.

"Mrs. Hearn? I'm Olga Marlin. Do you remember me? We met in Rome . . ."

She didn't give me a chance to say more. "What are you doing in Nairobi?" she nervously exclaimed. "We weren't expecting you till next week! This is terrible—there was no one to meet you! Stay right where you are, don't move! I'll inform the priests right away."

Shortly afterwards three cars pulled up, and the Opus Dei Counsellor and another priest emerged from one of them. They welcomed us and said how sorry they were that we had arrived before our telegram. "This is Monday, and still early in the morning, and the telegram may have been put in our post office box on Friday evening," explained the Counsellor. "We don't usually pick up mail on the weekend." How funny, I thought. I had always seen mail delivered at the door.

"I'm afraid your house is not quite ready," he went on, apologetically, "but I hope you will like it. If you'll get into the cars with Mrs. Hearn and Mrs. Lavelle, we'll meet you there."

I went with Agnes, who gave us a running commentary as we rode along. "Everything is very dry at present," she said, "because the rains have failed and we're in the middle of a drought."

In fact the dusty red earth was parched and cracked, with patches of flat yellow grass and here and there dry stalks of withered corn. The car raised clouds of red dust and every now and then we had to roll up the windows to keep it out. We passed a cluster of shops on the right. "This is Westlands," Agnes told us. "Magner's, the grocery store on the corner, is a family business where my brother works."

"What do you do?" I asked.

"I work as a secretary with a firm of auctioneers, but in fact I spend most of the time hunting for furniture and preparing the auctions. It's very interesting, but taxing."

At one point a red church spire came into view, surrounded by trees and buildings. "That's St. Austin's Catholic Church," Agnes said, "and now we're passing the girls' convent school, Loreto Msongari. Just behind it is St. Mary's, a boys' school run by the Holy Ghost Fathers. The schools are for Catholic European children, both boarders and day students. My daughter Maureen is finishing at Msongari this year. See the next ridge? That's where Strathmore College is being built."

We strained our eyes to find the college, but saw nothing on the rise in the terrain except bush and one solitary tree. "The foundations have been dug already," Agnes explained, "but you can't see anything from here."

I knew about Strathmore. The Father had told us that the men of Opus Dei were starting a prep school for boys which would be the first multiracial high school in Africa, and that they had met with open opposition. He stressed his constant teaching that out of a hundred souls we are interested in a hundred. "In the eyes of the Lord," he said, "there is no difference of nation, race, class, status . . . We're all brothers and sisters, and have to behave that way towards one another."

"My two sons," Agnes continued, "will be among the first students of the new school. I want them to mix with boys of other races, but without a lowering of academic or cultural standards. That is what people are afraid of. But Strathmore is aiming high and has enlisted an excellent team of teachers. Everyone is given an equal chance:

the selection of students is on a one-third European, one-third Asian, and one-third African basis. At first there was a lot of opposition, but now everyone is watching to see how they do."

I wondered how people would react to our multiracial finishing school for girls.

Agnes' voice broke in on my thoughts. "Here is the turn-in to your house." The three cars entered an uneven marram track with a signpost reading "Invergara Road." On either side were trees, bushes, and thick hedges, all covered with red dust. We passed Invergara Club, catching a glimpse of tennis courts, and soon afterwards turned onto a wide dusty drive encircling a small dry area in front of a sprawling gray stone bungalow with red-tiled roof. Here we stopped and everyone got out.

The front door opened immediately and a large Englishman appeared, clad in shorts and shirt, who looked around at us all with dismay. "I'm sorry," the Counsellor said to him, "but the girls arrived sooner than we expected." Then, turning to us, he explained, "This is Mr. Dave Bolland. He is making the altar for your oratory and had hoped to have it finished before you came." We shook hands and followed him into the house.

"Look at the beautiful floor!" exclaimed Mary, bending to touch it. It was dark brown parquet and shone like glass. The two ladies exchanged glances, and Agnes said, "We just finished waxing it."

The bungalow was shaped like a sideways horseshoe, with the front door in the middle and all along the head an enclosed veranda. In the center was a three-sided courtyard with direct access to the laundry and kitchen areas and leading to the garden.

It was a beautiful house. The large living room had a fireplace, a wall of glass windows, and a glass door that opened onto the wide, louvered veranda. The dining rooms, bedrooms, and bathrooms were accessed by a long, curved corridor. To the left from the front door another short corridor led to the oratory and then to a spacious kitchen, service, and laundry area with terrazzo floors. The pale yellow walls shone in the light streaming through the windows overlooking the courtyard.

"Who would have thought we would find such a lovely home waiting for us in Africa," Mary said in amazement.

Mrs. Lavelle showed us the furniture. "We only managed to get a few basic things so far," she said apologetically. "The bedrooms have beds, there's a set of sofas in the living room, and the ironing room has in it a bamboo wicker table and matching chairs. You may like to have your breakfast there, as it gets all the morning sun."

Before they left, Mrs. Hearn said, "I'll come over tomorrow in case you need anything, and we can set a day for me to take you shopping."

After they left, we didn't dare go outside. All the windows looked onto an enormous garden which disappeared into trees and bush. There was no other house in sight, so I thought we had no neighbors, and I half expected a lion or other wild animal to spring out from the shrubbery for a quick visit. It was several days before I realized that we were surrounded by many other houses set in compounds like ours—and that one had to go considerably out of one's way to find a lion. There were many things we had yet to learn about our new country.

We unpacked our things and carefully placed a framed photo of the Father on the mantelpiece in the living room, with a donkey in front of it.

At six-thirty the sun set, and by seven night had fallen. "That's how it is in the tropics," Marlene told us. "In the morning, you wake up in darkness and by the time you're dressed it's broad daylight. It was the same in Angola."

We dined on the provisions we had brought from Rome and then had a short get-together in the living room before going to bed. "We'd better go early," Mary said. "It's been an exciting day and no one got much sleep last night."

But the day's excitement hadn't ended. As we sat around the fireplace commenting on the day's events, the floor suddenly started shaking and the lights went out. "Madrecita!" cried Elisa in alarm. Then we all sat speechless until Mary finally said, "That was an earth tremor. We often had them in Japan." I had been prepared for lions and other wild animals, but this was totally unexpected. Apparently our new country was full of surprises.

7

Kenya High School

The next morning the Counsellor celebrated Mass for us in the unfinished oratory of the first women's center on the African continent.

That morning there were two phone calls. The first was for me, from Miss Thompson, principal of Kenya High School.

I had applied to teach at this government-run school rather than at a mission Catholic school simply because the spirit in which I had been formed was entirely lay— that of lay people struggling to bring the yeast of Christian holiness into whatever setting they found themselves in—a factory, hospital, public school, whatever. It was essential that from the outset this radically lay nature of our apostolate be clear, although at first it was difficult for many good, dedicated Catholics to understand it.

"Welcome to Kenya," Miss Thompson said warmly. "I have your teaching schedule here and would like to discuss it with you. As you know, we are already well into the second term, so if possible you should start teaching tomorrow. Do you have transportation?"

"No, I'm afraid not," I replied.

"Then let me call on you this afternoon and we'll work something out. You're at Monnas's place on Invergara Road, aren't you?"

The second call was from Mrs. Hearn, offering to take Mary shopping the next day. We still had enough food left to keep us going till then.

Mary and I got together to plan and divide out the work. "How much money do we have?" I asked. All told, we had 20,000 Italian lire and $295, which Mary could exchange at the bank.

"Who'll keep the accounts until Tere comes?" asked Mary. Tere was the secretary of the local council, and she had understood the bookkeeping classes Mary Ribero gave us at our workshop in Rome, whereas I had floundered. Mary Ribero had explained how to calculate the monthly kitchen average, and had stressed again and again the importance of double-entry bookkeeping.

"If you'll do the general accounts, I could look after the personal ones . . ." I said entreatingly. Mary, being better at accounting than I was, sighed and accepted the inevitable.

Miss Thompson came over that afternoon and showed me my schedule of classes and other duties at the school. I was to teach English, French . . . and math.

"I've never been any good at math!" I exclaimed.

"I'm so sorry, but I'm afraid it's too late to make any changes," Miss Thompson said. "You're a substitute teacher this term, and we just had to fill in the gaps. Take a look at the syllabus and select what you think you can handle. If you run into difficulties, the head of the math department, Mr. Brown, will give you a hand."

Then she went on to tell me about the school. "Kenya High is a European school," she said. "It was built for the children of settlers and of missionaries living in other parts of the country. Before, parents had to send their children to school in England, which was very expensive and meant being separated from them for long periods of time. Now Kenya High for girls and Prince of Wales and Duke of York for boys provide the same education the children would get in England. We are very proud of the high academic standards that have been set and maintained. We have over four hundred girls boarding in houses on the school compound, and there are cottages for the staff. You must come and have tea with me when you are settled."

Miss Thompson had arranged for a teacher who lived nearby to pick me up in the mornings. "If your schedules don't coincide some afternoons, you can always walk home, as the school is not very far away," she said before taking her leave.

I immediately went in search of Mary. "What will I do?" I groaned. "I'm supposed to teach math and I can't!"

Everyone was full of sympathy. "I would be nervous before the first day of school anyway, never mind having to teach an unfamiliar subject," said Marlene, shivering. "Will you be all right with the other classes?"

"I hope so. I don't have any books yet, so I haven't been able to get ready. Luckily my first class isn't till the end of the morning, so I can prepare it in the staff room."

"I hope you meet some nice girls. I want to start a club where we can teach crafts and introduce the girls to the Work," said Marlene, her dark eyes glowing.

"You can count on me for sewing classes," offered Elisa, "only we don't have a sewing machine." I glanced at Mary. We would also need one for the finishing school.

Rosario looked up and said, "You know what I'm thinking? We won't be able to look after the men's center until they move to Strathmore, but we could already take care of their laundry and oratory linens. I notice that the tray of the wicker table in the ironing room lifts off. We could put the things there and send them in the priest's car."

The idea was well received. "At the end of the month you can send us a bill covering expenses and salary," the priest said. So Rosario had a paid job at home.

When I returned to Invergara after my first day at Kenya High, everyone was eager to hear how it went.

"What about the math classes?" asked Mary, anxiously. "Will you be able to cope?"

"I talked to Mr. Brown, and he was very understanding. He agreed to let me concentrate on graphs, which I think I can handle. Luckily the girls haven't done them yet. I'll stretch the work out to fill all the periods. He promised to help me if I get stuck."

"What is the school like? Are the teachers nice?"

"Yes, but I felt very shy, being the only newcomer. Miss Thompson brought me into the staff room and introduced me to everyone. There are around fifty European men and women on the staff, all quite a lot older than me. Miss McDonald, the head of the English department, gave me my books and went over the syllabus with me."

"Did you meet any Africans?" asked Marlene.

"No. In fact, I felt as if I was teaching in an English school," I replied. "The only Africans around were the men who served morning coffee in the staff room, who are called 'boys,' and the gardeners, the 'shamba boys.'"

"Why are they called boys if they are men?" asked Elisa.

"That's what they call servants here. I didn't see any African women."

"Did you have lunch with the girls?"

"Yes. A teacher sits at every table. But between the clatter of the dishes and the noise of the girls it's practically impossible to carry on any conversation, which is a pity, because I would have liked to talk to Ann White, one of my French students. She told me her mother has been going to the monthly days of recollection given by an Opus Dei priest and was one of the ladies who helped get our house ready. Marlene, I think Ann will be interested in your club."

"That makes three girls so far," said Marlene, "because Mrs. Hearn's daughter Susan is coming with a friend, named Dorothy du Plessis. I'm longing for Tere to come so we can plan the classes together!"

The letters from Rome brought news of the travelers. Tere, Margaret, and Encarnación had already left on a boat for Mombasa, where they would board the train to Nairobi. The group going to Japan was still on the high seas. The Father had lit a candle in front of the stained-glass Madonna in the corridor of Villa Sacchetti, prayed for them, and said that a candle should remain burning there until they arrived safely at the port of Kobe. He had also asked Encarnita to make sure they would find letters waiting for them at every port of call.

Over the next weeks I became familiar with Kenya High and my responsibilities there. At the end of June I collected my salary and brought it home to Mary with a proposal: "What would you think of us sending this first salary to Rome?"

Mary's face brightened. "I think it's a wonderful idea! Their needs are greater than ours and we will manage without it."

* 8 *

Crisis in the Congo

On June 30, 1960, Belgium granted independence to the Congo, and in the staff room of Kenya High there was much heated discussion over it. The general opinion was that the transfer of authority from colonial power to an independent African government had been too sudden; that the Congolese were too bitterly divided for the situation to spell anything but disaster.

"They say the Africans are not ready for independence and there is bound to be trouble," I told the others at home that evening. "The British prime minister, Harold Macmillan, has caused a stir with his speech about the 'winds of change' sweeping the continent, and people are worried."

"Mrs. Hearn told me that here, too, the Africans are agitating for independence," put in Mary. "The leaders are calling for Kenyatta's release." She was referring to Jomo Kenyatta, the imprisoned leader of the Mau Mau freedom fighters, who had protested violently against the expropriation of so much of their land to the settlers.

"The teachers at Kenya High fear Kenyatta," I said. "They say that the governor called him 'a leader unto darkness and death,' and no one wants to stick around if he is set free. Miss McDonald asked me why I came to this country just when so many are thinking of leaving it."

"What did you tell her?"

"I said I want to get involved in the education of African women and am praying for peace in order to do it."

The forebodings of the Kenya High staff proved well founded. Six days later the Congo's Force Publique mutinied against their Belgian officers, and in the mutiny some European civilians were also killed. On July 11, in reprisal, the Belgian navy bombed the port of Matadi, and this sparked off violent revenge attacks on white people throughout the country.

When I arrived at school on Wednesday, July 13, the staff room was abuzz with harrowing stories of brutality to Belgian civilians in the Congo. As many as possible were being evacuated to neighboring countries, including Kenya.

"As of tomorrow Kenya High will be closed," the principal announced, "because the government needs emergency accommodations for a thousand refugees arriving by train and by air. All the girls are to stay home until further notice, except those who will be taking their school certificate and higher school certificate examinations at the end of the year." As I was teaching neither of those groups, this meant I would not be needed at school.

I was too engrossed in my own concerns to fully take in the importance of these events. I had been in Kenya for only a month, and my mind and heart were set on getting the Work started. Tere, Margaret, and Encarnación were arriving the following day, so I welcomed the break from school as a godsend.

Early the next morning Mary and I went to the railway station to meet them, in a used car we had just bought on credit: a cream-and-tan Fiat. It had taken some time to determine who could drive it.

Mary had been driving for many years, but wasn't confident driving on the left side of the road. As she didn't have an international license, she had to take the local driving test, and she failed. "I've been driving for fifteen years!" she told the examiner indignantly. "I drove all the way across the United States, from Boston to Los Angeles!" But he was adamant; she must try again three months later.

I, on the other hand, had a driver's license for Ireland that I had never used. I wrote to the driving school in Dublin asking them to send me an international one—although I wasn't sure they would, on account of what happened at the end of my last lesson. As we approached the school after a run through Phoenix Park and the lunchtime traffic, the instructor said, "Well done! Now just ease in here behind this vehicle . . ." and I accelerated instead of braking, ramming into the back of a parked truck . . . However, they did send me the license. So Mary drove, while I held the driver's license.

At last the huge black steam engine came puffing and whistling into the station, followed by a long line of shiny carriages, and soon we caught sight of the three waving from an open window.

"What's the matter with them?" Mary exclaimed. "They look terrible!" As soon as they descended I saw that the faces of all three were swollen and brick red.

After enthusiastic greetings, Tere explained that their boat had been delayed for many hours in sweltering heat at the Suez Canal because vessels headed for the Olympic games in Italy were being given priority. "It was like an oven," she said. "Poor Encarnación is covered with heat rash, so we should get her home as soon as possible."

"Mary has gone for the car and will pick us up at the entrance," I said, grasping one of the bags. "The trunks will be delivered later by truck."

"We already have a car?" asked Tere, astonished.

"Yes, and many other things. Wait till you see the house!"

Marlene, Rosario, and Elisa came running out to meet us as soon as the car pulled up. "Welcome to Invergara House!" "How was your journey?" "You're very red!"

"I think the three of them should go to bed," Mary told me. "They look exhausted. I'll get some powder for the heat rashes."

So it wasn't till after dinner that we were able to sit down together and hear the story of their adventures.

Tere began. "The Father blessed us before we left Rome," she said. "He said Africa is a marvelous continent and our work here will be a blessing from God.

"We went by train to Genoa, where we boarded the boat for Mombasa. None of us had ever traveled by boat before, so we were very excited. Luckily there was a priest among the passengers, so we had Mass every day, and we made ourselves a schedule combining pleasure and work. We studied English and Spanish every day and sewed tablecloths for the new house in Nairobi.

"We made friends with an African couple, Dr. and Mrs. Ang'awa. He had been studying in England and they were on their way home to Kenya. They have a little boy, whom I looked after when his mother got seasick."

"He really took to Tere," interposed Margaret. "You can see she's had plenty of experience with children."

"Well, what else can you expect with eleven younger brothers and sisters!" exclaimed Tere, laughing. "On the first day, I put my foot in it. I asked Dr. Ang'awa if he belonged to 'the Mau Mau tribe.' He was most amused. 'The Mau Mau are freedom fighters,' he explained. 'We are Luos from the province of Nyanza.' I felt like an ignoramus!" And she blushed at the memory.

"It was an English boat, so everything was very punctual and orderly. While we were waiting in Aden a British passenger said to Dr. Ang'awa, 'You must have some interesting tribal customs. Would you mind telling us about them?' The doctor replied courteously, 'I assure you, madam, that we have no tribal custom as curious as the British habit of dressing for dinner in the middle of the Red Sea.'"

Everyone laughed. "Did people really dress for dinner?" asked Rosario.

"Oh yes, every evening," Tere replied. "You could be

as casual as you liked during the day, but for dinner the men wore dinner jackets and the ladies put on evening dresses, or the best we had. We were also awakened every morning with 'morning tea' until I managed to persuade the steward that we really didn't want it, thank you! When the boat had docked, we were met by an English official, a friend of the Counsellor. Thanks to him, we quickly got through Customs. He took us to his home and we spent a quiet afternoon with him and his wife, sitting on the veranda, which overlooks the sea."

"The train trip was the best!" exclaimed Encarnación. "We saw zebras, antelopes, gazelles, ostriches, even a lion!"

"No!" cried the rest of us, enviously. "We haven't seen any animals yet."

"I can't understand how all those zebras are running loose," Encarnación went on, shaking her head. "In Catalonia, where I come from, we would have them in harness, doing something useful."

"Were you able to sleep on the train?" I asked.

"Oh yes. It's a pleasure to ride on that train," said Margaret. "We had our own compartment with comfortable seats that made up into beds at night. The dining car was paneled in mahogany and perfectly fitted out with plush seats. The tables were covered with spotless white linen and with silverware that had 'EAR&H'— East African Railways and Harbours—engraved on each piece. There was even a little vase of flowers on every table, and barefooted African waiters went noiselessly up and down, dressed in white robes and tall purple hats. They served us a four-course meal."

"That train was once known as the Lunatic Express," interposed Mary. "Mrs. Lavelle told me that everyone said, back at the turn of the century, that it was madness to try and lay a railway line from Mombasa to Lake Victoria. But they did it, despite all the dangers, including man-eating lions."

On that note we retired to bed, to dream of gleaming white beaches and trains chugging along between lions and harnessed zebras.

Early the following morning I was startled by Tere's voice.

"Olga, your father's on the phone!" she called excitedly.

"My father?" I hurried to the telephone in the hall, my heart thumping. "Daddy? Daddy, where are you?"

"Here in Nairobi! Don't you know there's a crisis in the Congo? I'm on my way from the High Commission for Refugees in Geneva to look into the situation, and I just thought I'd stop over in Nairobi to see my daughter."

"Oh, Daddy!" I cried, overwhelmed.

Suddenly Kenya didn't seem so far from home anymore. We had lunch at the Norfolk Hotel, and I told him about Kenya High and our plans for a multiracial finishing school. Afterwards I brought him to Invergara House, where he met all the others. He enjoyed practicing his Spanish with Tere.

We showed him around the house, which was still sparsely furnished. "Do you think you can get a piano in Nairobi?" Daddy asked. "If you find one, get it and I'll send you the money. What else do you need?"

"We were thinking of a bookcase for the study," Mary said diffidently. "We found in a magazine an attractive one that we thought could be copied. Would you like to see it?"

"Sure," answered Daddy. So Mary brought the picture. The bookcase had black metal bars with wooden shelves set at different levels. Daddy liked it. "Go ahead and have it made, it's a present from me," he said, making a face to hide his shyness.

My father was very interested in our plans. He later wrote to Mother: "Palais des Nations, Geneva, July 17, 1960 . . . I am proud of Olga really for what she is planning to do. She is actually in the front line, while I am in the rear directing a few troops. Whether or not it pleases everybody, the Africans are going to be independent and govern themselves, so the sooner they are educated and given the techniques for self-government, the better."

When the school reopened I returned to Kenya High, and met with a cool reception from the staff. Because I taught French they had expected me to turn up to translate for the refugees—something that had never occurred to me. Moreover, they were worried. There were rumors that Jomo Kenyatta was going to be set free and that Kenya would become another Congo. Many were talking of leaving the country.

9

A Call from the Father

"How many chairs do we need?" asked Mary. We were setting up the living room for a talk to be given for the ladies' monthly day of recollection. "I counted twelve ladies," I replied, "but some may arrive late, so we could set out three or four extra. I'm so happy that Ann White's mother, Rosemary, has come! The priest must be about to finish his talk in the oratory."

By now the Blessed Sacrament had been reserved in the tabernacle that the Father had shown us in Rome: a square one with jet stones. The tall black candlesticks stood on the varnished altar, which Mr. Bolland had finished the previous day. In gold lettering he had painted on the front "Consummati in Unum" (That they may all be one), words of Scripture (Jn 17:21) which the Father had used with reference to us, and which seemed particularly appropriate for our country.

A carefully packed cylinder arrived from Rome, and as soon as she saw it, Tere guessed what was in it. "The picture the Father promised us!" It was a triptych—three scenes from the life of the Virgin Mary. The central one had in the foreground a magnificent black king, in a green cloak and bright red stockings, waiting to offer a gold vessel to the Child.

"I'm sure the Africans will like it," mused Elisa. "Only we don't know any yet, except Nyawira."

It wasn't easy to meet Africans because in Nairobi the races were segregated. Buses were divided into two sections (the front for Europeans), and residential areas were also divided according to race. We lived in the European area called Lavington, Asians had their own areas, and Africans lived outside the city in "reserves."

Nyawira, a middle-aged Kikuyu woman, was our gardener. She came to us with the house. Her head was completely shaved, and she had long earlobes which she sometimes hooked onto the upper part of the ear, making a loop. Other times she used them to hold safety pins. On special occasions she filled the lobes to capacity with colorful beaded rings that stood out on either side of her head.

Her shiny skin was smooth and the color of milk chocolate. She wore, tied at the waist, a saffron-colored cloth that reached to just above her ankles, went under the arms, and draped around one shoulder. It had no stitches but was held in place with safety pins. She went barefoot.

Although she knew no English, she smiled and managed to carry on long conversations with Elisa, who was very intuitive. As Elisa spent a lot of her time working in the kitchen, which was by the garden, she saw Nyawira the most.

At first we looked gingerly at the "panga" which was Nyawira's gardening tool: a flat, wide steel knife with a wooden handle. But she maneuvered it very skillfully. I marveled that she never cut herself as she slashed the grass beneath her feet, lifting first one foot and then the other. After the day's work, Nyawira would go to the garden tap and rinse her head under the cool running water. Then she would hoist onto her shoulders a huge pile of wood that she had gathered and tied together with leather straps, and pull one strap over her forehead, which bore the brunt of the load resting on her bent back, and stagger away with a cheery "Niuguo tukonana ruciu" (Good-bye till tomorrow).

One day Nyawira alarmed Elisa by offering to shave off her hair with the panga so she could wash her head more easily! She was curious to know where we were from and how we came to Kenya, and Elisa discovered that the word for airplane is the same as for bird: "ndege." I noticed that every day, as soon as she arrived, Nyawira picked up a small stone and put it in a corner of the garden. The stones piled up as the days went by, till at the end of the month she collected them to show how many days she had worked and receive her wages.

When the school vacation began, Marlene started her club, with Susan Hearn, Ann White, Dorothy du Plessis, Tessa Ratclyffe, and Patricia Roche. The girls came to the house often, and every Saturday Father Joseph Gabiola gave them a talk in the oratory.

I wrote to the Father every week, and from Rome he followed with interest all that we were doing. Shortly after our arrival we received a letter from Encarnita asking for photos so that the Father could see where we were living. Wanting to show Invergara House at its best, we hired a professional photographer, from Elite Studios. A turbaned Indian came one afternoon, with an assistant carrying tripod and camera, and they took our first set of good photographs, which we proudly sent to Rome for the Father.

"We have to get the house ready for our school," Tere said nervously a few weeks after her arrival. "I'm very worried. It's due to open in five months and we have no furniture for the classrooms."

"Where do we get the money from?" asked Mary.

"We'll have to negotiate a loan from the bank and buy things at the auction," I said. "I'm sure Agnes Lavelle will help us."

The Ottoman Bank agreed to give us a three-year loan, and Tere and Marlene set about learning how to bid at the auctions, which were packed with the furniture of Europeans who were leaving the country.

They came home delighted with their bargains. "The sofa and these two armchairs went for nothing, just because the stuffing is coming out!" exclaimed Marlene. "We bought some thick cotton print in grays, blues, and beige to upholster them, and orange burlap to make curtains. The room will be very pretty."

"We also ordered the bookcase your father is giving us, and if you could draw a few ballerinas on the wall . . ." coaxed Tere. There was no denying her. I found myself copying three dancing figures in charcoal from a picture she gave me.

The visits to the auction multiplied, and soon the two could manage without the help of Mrs. Lavelle. One day they brought home an Underwood typewriter that Margaret called prehistoric, and a few days later, a manual Singer sewing machine bearing a metal plaque with the date 1886 on it. "First cousin of the typewriter!" sniffed Margaret in mock disdain.

But the sewing machine worked well, despite its antiquity, and soon rattled away producing curtains and covers under the steady hand of Encarnación, with Susan and Ann helping her. Dorothy, Tessa, and Patricia, under Tere's watchful eye, hammered in rows of tacks to upholster the sofa and chairs.

When the bookcase arrived, it filled the wall space beneath the ballerinas and soon displayed an artistic collection of books and knickknacks. Once all the furniture was in place, Susan stood at the door to admire the effect and then said with a sigh, "Isn't our room beautiful?"

"I saw a piano at the auction," Tere said to me a few days later. "Why don't you come and try it out? It's about time you did some shopping. We can go by car."

I found I could drive when I had to. After a few false starts, I got the car parked within easy walking distance of Bazaar Street and the Kurji Karsanji Auctioneers.

Bazaar Street seemed to have come straight out of India. Some of the *dukas* (shops) were open to the street and had standing in the doorway gunnysacks full of rice, dried beans, and interesting spices that filled the air with their aroma and tickled my nose. We passed turbaned men, some with beards tied up in a net. There were women in colorful silk saris and bright sandals, and occasionally one with a red dot on her forehead or a diamond in the nose.

The piano proved to be in good condition. "Let's hope we can get it," said Tere. "How nice it would look in the living room!" A couple of weeks later it arrived, and I started giving lessons.

Margaret found a job with a real estate agency called Tyson's, and always came home from work with the paper and the latest news from town. Before long she had made several good friends, and one of them, Anne King, came to Invergara for the monthly days of recollection.

"All the secretaries are Europeans," Margaret told us. "Most of them are wives of government officials or businessmen. You don't see any African women in town, except at the market."

Mary's hours at the Fairfield Nursing Home varied. Sometimes she had night duty and came home to sleep during the day. She was looking after elderly European people and, like Margaret, earning a good salary.

The Counsellor and another priest met with us regularly to see how we were doing, give us advice, and share with us what they had learned by experience. On one of these occasions Father Joseph Gabiola offered to introduce me to Jemimah Gecaga, the first African woman on the Legislative Council. "She's not Catholic," he said, "but she is a good Christian and very interested in what you have come to do."

Mrs. Gecaga was a Kikuyu lady related to Jomo Kenyatta. A small woman, she had eyes that missed nothing, and what she saw would swiftly be translated into an approving smile or stern disapproval. She had a distinct air of authority and great dignity. From our first meeting I conceived a great respect for her. She already knew about Opus Dei through her contact with Father Joseph, and she became a friend and mentor.

Mrs. Gecaga had a strong sense of justice, and her main concern at the time we met was political freedom for the African people—a close ally to the emancipation of women.

"You have arrived at a very good time to open a school for girls," she told me. "Our women need education in order to become self-reliant, respect themselves, and make themselves respected. This can only happen when they are financially independent. Your school should provide them with the necessary skills."

I talked this over later with Tere and Mary. "Do you think our students will be able to earn money with what we teach them?" I asked.

"Well," Tere answered, "they'll learn sewing and crafts." Then she added thoughtfully, "But I see what Mrs. Gecaga means. She wants African women to be employable."

"But we don't yet have any African girls for our school," Mary pointed out.

That, unfortunately, was true. Susan Hearn, Dorothy du Plessis, Tessa Ratclyffe, Patricia O'Shea, Marlene and Imelda Hanrahan, Elvira Tonolo, Heather Darling, and Patricia Roche had applied, and more were expected to apply before the end of the year, but they were all Europeans.

I told Mrs. Gecaga this when I next visited her, but she wasn't fazed. "The different communities are segregated," she said, "and so are the schools, but when we get independence this will change. It is important for the country that Kenyatta be released as soon as possible so that he can lead us into self-rule. We need him. My brother Dr. Njoroge Mungai has given up his medical practice to join other African leaders in the struggle to bring him home. Meanwhile, be patient. Soon you will have more African girls in your school than you can cope with!"

It was Agnes Lavelle who first suggested putting secretarial studies in our curriculum. "Some mothers have asked me if you intend to offer shorthand and typing," she said, "because they want their daughters to be able to get jobs afterwards. Why don't you think about including these skills in your program?"

"I don't know anything about them," I said doubtfully, "but Margaret is a secretary. I'll talk it over with her."

Later on I discussed Agnes' idea with the others. "I don't see how we can train secretaries," I said. "It's not what we're prepared for and most of us have no experience in secretarial work."

After a moment's silence Tere said firmly, "I like the idea. We have to be open-minded, Olga, and not only will this satisfy those mothers, but we will also be able to offer African girls the kind of training Mrs. Gecaga was talking about."

I had to admit she was right. "How do we go about it, then?" I asked.

"I can teach typing," volunteered Margaret, "but we'll have to find a Pitman Shorthand teacher. I learned Gregg, and here the government insists on Pitman certificates. Why don't you talk to the principal of one of the secretarial colleges, Olga? She may be able to advise us."

I made an appointment with the principal of a well-established college in town and told her what we were planning to do. She confirmed that only applicants with Pitman Shorthand certificates from London were considered for employment, but didn't know of any teacher who was looking for a job.

"There's a Pitman representative in Nairobi who gives the exams and forwards them to London . . . but surely you don't expect *African* girls to pass those exams, do you?" she asked incredulously. I left her office feeling deflated and out on a limb. We were plunging into courses I knew nothing about and committing ourselves to turn out African girls who could succeed.

Tere made calculations. "If we get eight typewriters, we can admit twenty-four students, so that they each have two hours of typing practice and the machines are never idle. But where will we find the money?"

Mary Mahoney came to the rescue. "In the hospital I worked at in the United States," she said, "I have retirement money accumulating that can be drawn out at any time, so why don't I claim it now?" She did, and with that we bought eight new typewriters, and Margaret prepared to teach.

One evening Mrs. Gecaga invited me to go with her to the Parliament Building, where the Legislative Council met. We entered the spacious lobby, where parliamentarians in business suits were moving about greeting one another or standing in groups holding animated conversations. She smiled and nodded at several people and then said, "Come, I'll introduce you to Tom Mboya." I was awed at the prospect of meeting the elected secretary general of the newly formed Kenya African National Union, and followed Mrs. Gecaga timidly.

We walked across to where a stocky, very black young man stood talking with several other African gentlemen. He had a round face with a serious expression and narrow, penetrating eyes beneath a sloping forehead. "Let me introduce this young woman to you," she said. "She is an American and has come with several other ladies to start a multiracial finishing school for girls in Nairobi. Perhaps you may be able to assist them."

Mr. Mboya turned to me with a half-smile and nodded courteously as we shook hands. "I'm very glad to hear it," he said. "There is need for a school of that kind. I wish you every success." Then he added, "When you get started I'll certainly send you some students."

The Father spent the summer of 1960 in London, and one day an envelope arrived bearing English stamps and addressed in Encarnita's handwriting. She was asking for our telephone number. "Wouldn't it be wonderful if you could talk to the Father?" she wrote.

From then on we dreamt of that phone call. In the

evening get-togethers Tere took out a stopwatch and we practiced to see how much could be said in three minutes, with everyone getting to say something.

One day Mrs. Gecaga brought Mary and me to a women's meeting at the newly formed United Kenya Club. It was the first time that women from all races were coming together. One could sense the exciting upsurge towards independence and nationhood, and the ardent desires of these women to create a new, free society devoid of any discrimination.

Among the few Europeans lobbying for a united Kenya was Mrs. Dorothy Hughes, Legislative Council member for Uasin Gisu. On July 13, 1960, in an interview, she said, "To compare the happenings in the Congo to what will happen when independence comes to Kenya is ridiculous and incorrect. Europeans who by quiet example mean to stay and develop farms and build homes and businesses are the true voice of Kenya. Any other attitude does a great disservice to the European community and an even greater disservice to those Africans whom we look on as our colleagues and friends."

I met Dorothy shortly after our arrival in Kenya, when I telephoned Mr. John Hughes and was invited to their home for tea.

Mary and I went together. Built on a hill near St. Austin's, the Hughes' home had an impressive entrance, with wrought-iron gates, and a broad tarmacked driveway lined on both sides with trees that led to sunken gardens containing tropical plants. The grounds spread out wide on either side with jacaranda trees and bougainvillea tables.

I rapped timidly with the brass knocker, and the door was opened by a small, fair-haired woman with freckles and a hospitable manner.

"Come in," she said cheerily. "My husband is expecting you." She ushered us into a large, comfortable living room, artistically furnished, with a magnificent view of the gardens from a window that filled that whole end of the room. John Hughes was a large, florid Irishman who was now a Ford dealer with a thriving business in Kenya.

"Glad to meet you," he said jovially, putting out his hand. "How's Digby?" I told him the little I knew, while Dorothy poured us some tea.

"Are those your children?" asked Mary, looking with interest at the pastel portraits on the wall.

"Yes, we have six," Mr. Hughes said. Then he added proudly, "My wife is also an architect."

"How did you come to Kenya?" I asked Dorothy.

"My family came up from South Africa in an oxcart when I was three," she said, "and they settled in Eldoret, where we had a farm. Later I went to school in England and studied architecture there, but my heart was in Kenya." Then she asked, "What brought you to this country?"

I explained about Opus Dei and our plans for a multi-racial secretarial-cum-finishing school, and she was very interested. "Independence is going to come sooner than people think, and we'll need educated Africans," she said. "I'm so glad you intend to work with African women—they have had a very rough deal."

Besides running her architectural firm and serving on the Legislative Council, Dorothy also worked on a number of social service committees. She was a convert to Catholicism. She soon began to attend the monthly days of recollection at Invergara and eventually became a co-operator of Opus Dei, meaning that she helped with her professional advice, prayer, and financial assistance, while sharing in all the spiritual benefits of Opus Dei.

On Thursday, September 1, it rained all evening, and at 7:00 the electricity went out. Just then the phone rang. Tere groped her way to it, picked up the receiver, and heard the operator say, "We have a call for you from your father." Knowing immediately who it was, she shouted for everyone to come. In the darkness and commotion everything we had so carefully written down was forgotten, as the Father's voice came over the line, warm and vibrant. He asked how we were, and wanted to speak to each one in turn. Then, after encouraging us to be faithful, he sent us his blessing. We could only chorus, "Thank you, Father, thank you!" After that, Encarnita spoke to us for a moment. "Write to the Father about everything, write to him often," she said. "He is always asking about you."

We put down the receiver and remained standing there, overwhelmed. Later we learned that the Father had called the women in Japan that same evening. Intercontinental calls were rare and expensive, and we could only guess at the sacrifices that had gone into making possible these little calls that had given us such joy and encouragement.

10

First Experiences

One of our first excursions outside Nairobi was to Loreto Convent in Limuru, where the Sisters ran a secondary boarding school for African girls. It was one of the few schools in the country where they could study for the Cambridge School Certificate. The car climbed most of the way, as the mission was high in the hills, nestled among tea and coffee estates. Tere and I were met at the convent door by the principal, Mother Colombier, a tall, dynamic Irishwoman. She welcomed us in to a cup of tea and listened attentively to the plans for our school.

"You have to realize that not many African girls go to secondary school," she cautioned. "Usually they are married off as soon as they graduate from primary school, or even before. Those who finish the eight years at school sit for the Kenya African Primary Education Certificate, whereas European and Asian children spend only seven years in primary school and follow a different curriculum which leads to the Kenya Primary Education Certificate. The idea is to give African children the advantage of an extra year of formal education, as so few will continue. They generally start school much later than children of other communities, so it is quite common for an African child to finish primary school at eighteen or twenty."

"How old are the girls when they get married?" asked Tere.

"That will depend on their fathers, but often they may be fifteen or sixteen."

"Then how do you get students for this school?" I asked, remembering the girls I had seen around the compound in bright red jumpers and white blouses.

"Things are slowly changing," Mother Colombier said, "and we are trying to encourage parents to send their daughters to secondary school. The girls are very keen. We have some good students here, and they are aware of the responsibility they have to do well so as to pave the way for others."

"Do you think any of the girls would be interested in a secretarial career?" asked Tere. "We're planning to start a vocational school."

Mother Colombier thought for a while and then said, "I don't want to discourage you, but you have to keep in mind that most of the families don't have the money to pay tuition. Moreover, it will be difficult to convince fathers that their daughters will be safe, working in offices with men."

Those were serious difficulties, and Tere and I discussed them as we drove away, without reaching any conclusions.

As Limuru is seventeen miles outside Nairobi, we had packed sandwiches and decided to look for a nice spot to picnic before returning home. Along Ngong Road we came upon Langata Forest. It was a thin forest, with tall, sparse trees and inviting flat spaces in between, so we parked on the tarmac road beside it, headed for a nice clearing, and sat down to eat our lunch. It was a pleasant place.

Suddenly, out of nowhere, just as we had finished, an elderly African man appeared, wearing a long beige gabardine and brandishing a panga! He grabbed my pullover, Tere's purse, and some other things, and ran away. I was petrified, but Tere ran after him in great indignation. I shouted frantically, "Tere, come back, come back!" fearing that the man would turn on her. At last she gave up and came back, furious. We stood in our stockings, having lost our shoes in the fracas, and took stock of the situation. The car was still there, but at risk since the keys were in the purse.

We walked helplessly to the main road, and almost immediately an English lady pulled over. We explained what had happened and asked if she would take us home to pick up the other set of car keys, and she kindly did so. We crept stealthily into the house so as not to alarm anyone, collected shoes and car keys, and went with the lady back to our car. Before leaving us she said, "You must report the theft immediately at the police station," and pointed to a whitewashed office bungalow just down the road.

When we told the police officer our story, he was horrified. "Madam," he said, "do you mean to say that you *picnicked* in Langata Forest? Why, the place is notorious! Any number of men could have come down upon you, and anything might have happened! You were very lucky."

Early the next morning an agitated Agnes Lavelle telephoned, saying, "What is this I have just read in today's paper?" The whole episode had appeared in the newspaper, with full names.

Christmas was approaching and we still hadn't found a shorthand teacher. No one wanted to leave a well-paid job to go into teaching, let alone in a new school, so Agnes offered to teach me after work. We spent many hours going over the Pitman manual, but that still didn't turn me into a shorthand teacher.

"It's hard to believe Christmas is around the corner," said Mary, fanning herself. The weather continued to be hot, dry, and dusty during the day, though at night it could become quite chilly on account of the altitude.

"Marlene and I saw our first Christmas decoration in Nairobi today. An Indian butcher has written 'Merry Xmas' in cotton wool on the inside of his shop window," Tere told us. "I wrote to tell my mother about it. I have only seen one small Nativity set, in the Alitalia window. I've never had Christmas without a Nativity set."

"Neither have I," I said, and I thought nostalgically of

Mother's clay figures that we carefully unpacked every year and placed in a wooden stable on a table in the living room that was draped in a white sheet covered with plumped-up, glitter-sprinkled cotton wool.

We made our own decorations for Invergara House with silver-painted dry branches and colorful leaves. Margaret and Encarnación disappeared into the kitchen, where no one else was allowed to enter, while Tere and Marlene occupied the living room, where, constantly threatened with interruption, they sewed presents for everyone.

Early in the morning of Christmas Eve there was a phone call for Tere from Embakasi Airport. "We have a package for you," the official said, "with instructions that it should be picked up today."

Tere drove off right away, accompanied by Mary, while the rest of us waited, full of curiosity. They returned with a big box that had "Fragile" written all over it. Inside were thirty little figures for the Nativity set! Tere's mother had bought them and had sent the package with a Nairobi-bound pilot so they would be sure to arrive on time for Christmas.

We took them out and reverently unwrapped them, one by one. All the familiar figures were there: the Holy Family, the Three Wise Men, angels, shepherds, sheep, washerwomen, even Herod in his palace. We stood looking at them silently. The Nativity set had come to us in Africa. No matter that the sun was beating down from a cloudless sky and the earth lying parched and dry outside, while in Ireland wind and rain howled outside the house and in Canada snow lay several feet deep . . . Christmas was Christmas!

We happily collected bark and straw from the garden to make the stable, strewed earth around it, then arranged banana leaves on either side, and Mary affixed a little bulb in a corner. We put all the figures in place and then stood back to admire the effect.

"It's lovely," Rosario said, heaving a deep sigh of satisfaction. "Now Christmas is really here."

Some of our friends came to visit over the Christmas holidays, among them Mrs. Hannah Rubia and her six children. Mrs. Gecaga had taken me to visit the Rubias in Kangemi, where they lived in a good stone house in the middle of the reserve, surrounded by traditional huts and shacks.

Mr. Charles Rubia introduced me to his wife with evident pride. A small, gentle woman with a kindly face and capable manner, she took an immediate interest in our plans for a multiracial school.

"It is urgent for our women to get an education," she said. "They need to learn how to run a modern home, to speak English, and to relate with people of other races. When we obtain our independence, they will have to manage their homes and entertain at the level of their husbands' positions. We built a good house here in the middle of the reserve on purpose to show other families that it can be done and to motivate them to raise their own standard of living."

During that Christmas season some of Hannah's neighbors came to Invergara asking to "see your Bethlehem," and so our circle of African friends widened.

When the season was over we carefully packed away the Nativity set and the decorations, among them a silver-painted branch from a frangipani bush. Some months later I opened the box only to find to my amazement that the silver branch had sprouted green leaves and was beginning to flower! I took the brave little shoot outside and planted it.

Our school was due to open on January 13 of the new year, 1961. We had prepared the secretarial and home economics courses and had turned our bedrooms into classrooms by using collapsible beds that could disappear into a closet during the day and by buying portable chair desks. But still we had no teacher for the most prestigious subject in the secretarial section. We advertised, and made inquiries among our friends, but without success.

"What are we going to do?" I asked in desperation, looking around at the others. "The school opens in ten days!"

"You'll just have to fill in yourself till we find a teacher," said Margaret.

"That won't do," I said. "The girls will lose confidence in the school and leave. There's a lot of competition among secretarial colleges, and one of the mothers told me they were advised not to send their daughters to be guinea pigs in a new school."

Margaret looked up, startled, but didn't say anything. She just frowned and clamped her lips together in a look of dogged determination.

The following evening she announced triumphantly, "I've got a shorthand teacher!"

"Who? How?" asked Tere, amazed.

"Her name is Audrey Leitch. She's an English colleague of mine at Tyson's. She knew that I was leaving to teach typing in our new school and that we're in a bind for lack of a Pitman Shorthand teacher. Today I asked her if she would come and be our shorthand teacher . . . and she agreed!"

"Hurray!" we all cried, hugging Margaret.

"There's one condition," she went on. "She wants to bring her baby with her. I promised her this would be no problem. Do you realize she will forfeit a month's pay, and the salary we can pay is much lower?"

Very grateful to Audrey, we now got ready to open our school with a full quota of staff.

Seventeen students had been admitted, but they were all Europeans. Only one non-European had applied: a Goan girl. When we went to register the school with the city's education department, I was told that before a nonwhite could be admitted to a school in our residential area we had to get the written permission of all our neighbors. Tere and I drew up a letter and brought it from house to house—but everyone refused to sign!

I had to call the girl's mother to say that we could not admit her daughter. It was against everything we stood for, and I felt dreadful. The lady simply said, in a dry voice, "I quite understand," and hung up. Eventually this lady became a member of Opus Dei, and her granddaughter was among the first students at Kianda Secondary School. But that was many years later.

Meanwhile we had to get another place as soon as possible where we could admit girls of all races. "Where can that be, with the city segregated?" I asked Tere.

"Let's talk to Mr. Roche," she suggested. "He owns a real estate agency in Westlands, and I'm sure he can help us." Good-natured Irishman that he was, Paddy Roche took our problem to heart and promised to look for something suitable.

Mrs. Lavelle also tried to help. She showed us a property for sale on Valley Road, very near the Nairobi City Center. It was so well located that for a while we pictured ourselves there, and when it came to deciding on a name for the school, I looked up "valley" in the Kikuyu dictionary and found the word "kianda." As it turned out, the property on Valley Road was far beyond our means, but we liked the name and kept it. I asked Mrs. Gecaga what she thought of it, and she liked it very much. "Kianda is a perfect name for a school," she said, "because it means a valley where everything you plant grows strongly and well."

"Do you need any help?" Tere asked on the eve of the first day of school, looking into the typing room, where Margaret was placing a gray plastic cover on the last typewriter. "I think everything's ready now," Margaret replied, raising a flushed face. "I'm nervous about starting teaching tomorrow, aren't you?"

"Yes," answered Tere. "It's scary beginning something new. But we know some of the girls already, which will make it easier. Come look at the shorthand room."

The large bedroom at the end of the corridor had been transformed and now contained neat rows of chair desks for the shorthand students. Sewing and crafts would be taught in the room with the bright orange curtains, the bookcase, and the painted-on-the-wall ballerinas. Along the veranda there were tables and chairs for the language and general-knowledge classes.

"Why don't we give the girls a questionnaire to fill out when they come tomorrow," I proposed. "That could be a good way of getting to know them." So we put our heads together and compiled a set of questions that would give us an idea of the backgrounds and interests of our students.

The next morning, parents were already dropping off their daughters by seven, although school didn't start till eight. Audrey Leitch arrived with her baby, Andrew, and he lay happily in a little hammock hanging from the branch of a tree, under the watchful eye of Elisa.

"Tere," Susan called out, "come show Elvira the 'sleepy doll' we made." So Tere brought out a doll made of pink corduroy which zipped up the back to hold a nightie. It had a cute face, with black felt lashes, a button nose, and a pursed mouth. "What lovely soft hair!" exclaimed Elvira, stroking the beige and white fur that stuck out of the corduroy hood, which finished in a pom-pom. "It's a scrap of antelope skin they gave me in a shop," Tere told her. "I found astrakhan for the African dolls. We made lots of them at Christmas and Mrs. Erica Boswell sold them for us in her shop." At Jax, a trendy clothes shop across from the New Stanley Hotel, Erica sold garments she herself had designed. Our dolls of all complexions—black, white, brown—lay, thumb in mouth, in the shop window, and sold well. "You'll learn how to make them in the crafts classes," Tere told Elvira, putting the doll back on its shelf.

By eight all the girls had arrived, dressed in full cotton frocks over fashionable petticoats, and they greeted one another enthusiastically. The house was full of blondes, with two exceptions: Elvira, who was Italian, and Rosemary Homan, who also had black hair. Tere marshaled all the girls into their respective classrooms and soon everything was quiet as they sat sucking on their pens, thinking out their answers to the questionnaire.

The girls were lively and the atmosphere was warm and friendly. They called us by our first names and soon were part of the household. Dorothy, Susan, and Elvira were Catholic and came early to go to Mass with us, and afterwards they helped put everything away. Dorothy came to Invergara every day on a *piki-piki* (motorbike). Her family was from South Africa and she had lived all her life in Africa, so she could tell us the names of trees, flowers, and birds.

Paddy Roche was as good as his word. One morning he phoned to say, "I think I have found just the right place for you. If you'll meet me at my office, I'll take you there." Tere and I set out right away and followed him along Sclater's Road—the main Nairobi-Nakuru road—onto Churchill Avenue, where we took the first turn to the right.

A narrow avenue lined with trees, tropical plants, and flowers led to a traffic island with a big jacaranda tree in full bloom and beneath it a carpet of purple flowers. Near the island was a gray stone bungalow built in the colonial style, with low ceilings, small windows set in wooden frames, and a red corrugated iron roof. It stood on five acres of land. From the front veranda we could see on the opposite ridge the African huts which marked the beginning of the Kangemi Reserve, and far in the distance the Ngong Hills clearly outlined against the horizon.

"It's lovely, but isn't this a European area?" I asked.

"Yes, it is," Paddy replied. "That's the amazing thing.

You're in luck. I inquired about this property at the Nairobi City Council, and the official I spoke to discovered that it is one of several around the Japanese consulate which were designated multiracial out of deference to the consul."

We liked the property very much, and speculated on the alterations that would have to be made to adapt the bungalow for use as home and school. The European owner was eager to sell, as she was uncertain about the future and planned to leave the country, so it was going at bargain price.

In order to establish ownership, Tere and I talked with a lawyer, Mr. Frank Addly. "What do you propose to set up?" he asked in a businesslike tone of voice. "A trust, a company limited by guarantee . . . ?" We looked at one another blankly. Mr. Addly, peering at us over his glasses, broke into a smile and said, "I would advise you to set up an educational trust with three of you as the first trustees." He drew up the Kianda Foundation Trust Deed, creating a nonprofit educational trust for the promotion of the educational, social, and spiritual welfare of women in Kenya, to hold the new Kianda property and other future projects. Into this trust would go everything we could beg, borrow, and save.

Now we were in a position to start our school in earnest.

11

Creating a Home

From Invergara it was a twenty-minute walk through the bush to a spot where we could see the progress of Strathmore College. "It's unbelievable!" Mary exclaimed. "The building is already up." This was January (of 1961), and the Strathmore College of Arts and Sciences was due to open on March 7.

It was the beginning of another venture. The women of Opus Dei were going to look after the catering services for the staff and students of the new college, while training African girls.

Word quickly got around of what we were planning to do, and our European friends told us we were crazy. "African women know nothing about a modern house," said one. "They can't learn, they'll run away," warned another. Even Agnes Lavelle, who supported everything we did, was skeptical. "We have always had houseboys," she said, "and the City Council requires every house to provide quarters for them. It's the normal thing."

But we had come to work with women.

The Counsellor told us about Consolata Mission in Tetu, Nyeri, where the nuns had a home crafts school for African girls. "The Sisters have been working there for years," he said. "They have a lot of experience and will be able to advise you."

Mary and I spent a day at the mission. The Sisters were teaching household skills to primary school leavers. Sister Germana showed us around the compound, where the young women were learning cooking, sewing, and agriculture. The quadrangles consisted of single-story rows of cement-floored classrooms and dormitories—simple, functional, and clean—and were set in lush gardens over-hung with flowering trees and bushes.

Sister Germana invited us for lunch, and afterwards Mary and I told her about our plans for Strathmore and the skepticism we had met with. She shook her head. "Those women were wrong," she said, much to my relief. "The African girls are hard workers, and you'll see how quickly they will learn. Moreover, the houseboy system should be discouraged. It's bad for the family, because the men end up having one wife up-country in the village and another in their quarters in town."

Then she said, "If the first girls like the training, others will follow. I'll talk about it to the girls about to finish our course, and if any of them want to work with you, I'll encourage their fathers to send them."

I also talked to Mrs. Rubia, and she was very excited about the project since it coincided with her own desires to educate women in the care of the home. She promised to look for suitable girls.

"I would like to visit the place," she said, "with some friends who could also help." We set up a time, and Mary and I showed Jemimah Gecaga, Margaret Kenyatta, Mrs. James Gichuru, and Hannah Rubia around the future catering unit. Although the building was still under scaffoldings, they were very impressed with everything.

"Do you mean the girls will live in the same house with you?" Mrs. Gichuru asked incredulously. "Yes, of course," Mary replied. "We are a family, and they will be part of it."

Shortly afterwards we received a letter from Sister Germana saying that four girls from the Tetu mission were ready to work with us. We only needed to tell them when to come and what to bring with them. Mrs. Rubia had also found two girls for us, so we could count on six trainees.

While we were trying to figure out how to cope with both Kianda and the catering department of Strathmore, news arrived from Rome. The Father was sending three more women to Kenya for Strathmore! They were María de los Angeles (known as Cuca) Canel, who would be coming from Spain; Obduli Martín, from Rome; and Carlota Díaz, from England. Mary, because she already knew something about the country, would move to Strathmore with them, Marlene taking her place in the local council of Invergara. The three were traveling to Kenya on February 21, so we wrote to Sister Germana asking that the girls come on February 22.

Encarnación and I went to meet the newcomers at the airport, but though we arrived in good time, we found them waiting for us. After enthusiastic embraces, Cuca launched into an account of their adventures as we made our way to the car.

"We missed the plane, that's why we're so early. We traveled on a nonstop South African flight which got here before the British Airways one. It was because of the paintings . . ."

"The Father sent a triptych for our oratory!" put in Obduli, beaming at me. She was a small, dynamic woman from Seville with whom I had worked in the servery of Villa Sacchetti, in Rome. "The customs officers opened the cylinder in Fiumicino," she said, "so we were able to see it—a Madonna and Child with two chubby angels on either side, one black and one white."

"That was what delayed us," took up Cuca, eager to get on with her story. "Some old masters were stolen and smuggled out of Italy a few weeks ago, and the customs officers were suspicious, especially since the central panel is still wet and was done on a used canvas. They took it away and scratched off some of the paint underneath for analysis. We said we were going to miss our plane, but they didn't care. By the time the picture was cleared it was too late, the plane had left. They were very apologetic and promised to put us on the next plane to Africa—and then they treated us to a first-class dinner, all to ourselves, at two in the morning. And to top it all, we arrived before the scheduled flight!" Cuca's dark eyes shone with glee over the good outcome of their adventure.

As soon as the car arrived at Invergara, everyone ran out with cries of welcome. Rosario and Elisa smothered Obduli in hugs, while Tere cried excitedly, "Cuca! Who could have told us we would meet again in Kenya!" and Margaret grabbed hold of Carlota and plied her with questions about the people she had left in England. When the noise subsided a little, Mary asked, "How is the Father? Did you see him?"

"Oh yes," cried Cuca, "we spent ten days in Rome! And yesterday the Father celebrated Mass for us in his oratory and told us he was offering it for us. We saw him several times, and he sent all of you his blessing. He knows everything you're doing here. Before we left he reminded us that we should become one with the people of this country."

That same afternoon Josephine Nyakarundu, Euphrasia Wagiatha, Esther Nyaguthie, and Veronica Wambui arrived by bus from Tetu, while Mrs. Rubia brought Mary Nyambura and Veneranda Wanjiru. Veronica had no shoes, so I gave her a pair of mine—blue slip-ons I had bought with Pilarín in Ireland. It was her first time to wear shoes, and these were narrow at the toe, so she shuffled along for some time until she could manage to lift her feet.

That night they slept in the unfinished building at Strathmore, on top of piled-up mattresses, and in the morning returned to Invergara, since workers were still all over the place during the day. It wasn't until February 25 that they were able to move into their new building and get organized.

They had an important work to do. Much of what makes Opus Dei a family, and all its centers family homes, is the skill and dedication of those women who make hospitality their profession and spend themselves looking after the others. The founder's mother and his sister Carmen looked after the first Opus Dei center and created an elegant family home in the midst of postwar poverty and privations. They set a tradition which Carmen taught to the first women who came to the Work and which, as a rule, would be carefully maintained in all the centers throughout the world.

The Father set great store by this work, calling it "the apostolate of apostolates" because of its importance to people's well-being, both physical and spiritual. He often reminded us that everyone receiving these services should be able to discern behind them the caring hand of their mother, their older sister...the Blessed Virgin Mary herself. Now it was our responsibility to make this a reality at Strathmore for the seventy-five students and staff members who would be living there.

The newcomers spent the first days learning their way around the sprawling three-story building, which stretched along all four sides of a large courtyard that was to become the physical center and hub of the day's activities. Paved with red quarry tiles, it was full of light, as the sun shone there all day long. A grassy patch in front of the gray stone façade of the trainees' dining room was filled with tropical plants, cacti, flowers, and a couple of newly planted trees. The kitchen, laundry, ironing room, and servery opened onto the courtyard, as also did one floor of cubicles for the trainees. The walls were painted white and the woodwork red, so the general effect was bright and cheerful. Communication was very easy; one could just stand in the courtyard and call out a message.

The girls had never seen a staircase before. Nor had they ever used basic cleaning equipment or handled silverware and china. Now they had to learn about refrigerated rooms, potato peelers, deep fryers, gas and electric ovens, dishwashers, washing machines, and the intricacies of an Aga cooker, which functioned with anthracite. In the mission school they had only learned to cook on *jikos*—portable tin charcoal stoves.

Carlota ran the kitchen with the help of Mary Nyambura and Josephine Nyakarundu. One afternoon Mary asked Carlota, "Will you please tell me when five minutes are up?" (None of the girls had watches.) "Yes," replied Carlota, "but why do you ask?" "I want to see how many French fries I can cook in five minutes, so I'll know what time to start frying the potatoes for dinner." These were the so-called untrainable girls.

The trainees took to sitting in the courtyard on stools to shell peas or sift rice, and buckets and mops were laid out on the tiled floor to dry. But at other times the court-yard became the scene of lively recreational sessions in which they wrapped colorful *kangas* (bright cotton squares) around their waists, tied strings of bottle tops or of squashed tin cans with stones inside around their ankles, and, stamping their feet, swayed and bent, singing and gesticulating rhythmically to the sound of the "drum beat" coming from the metal drains in the servery.

The courtyard was also witness to a culture clash. Cuca had been given a bag of wrapped candies, and she decided to give the girls a surprise. In the evening, while they were dancing, she went to a window and called out to them, and when they looked up, she showered them with candies. Instead of showing delight, the girls stopped dead, turned on their heels, and walked away, leaving the candies on the ground. "What happened?" asked Cuca, wide-eyed. There was no answer, no one would speak to her, till finally Josephine told her angrily, "Food is only thrown to animals!"

Another day Euphrasia started a strike and the others joined in. No one would get up. They wouldn't work and they wouldn't talk, except among themselves and in Kikuyu. Cuca couldn't think what was the matter until Josephine, who was the eldest and one of the more mature, told her, bashfully, that they had been wondering why they were being treated so well and had concluded that there must be something unsavory behind it. After that Josephine defused the strike and things went back to normal.

On Saturday afternoons the girls would go out to the garden, sit on the grass, and do some sewing or fix each other's hair. They produced real works of art, one sitting with legs outstretched and the other kneeling over her pulling the hair straight with a long-handled wooden comb and then braiding it into hundreds of tiny plaits.

Cuca wanted to celebrate the girls' birthdays, but none of the trainees knew her date of birth. There was no such thing as a birth certificate. People identified the year they were born by some important event that had occurred around the same time and that might even be incorporated into their name, like a great flood or drought, a bumper harvest, the death of an important person, the arrival of an outstanding visitor . . . After Queen Elizabeth II visited Nyeri in 1952, for example, many children were named "Queen."

When Cuca realized there were no birthdays to celebrate, she suggested the alternative of the saint's day, since all the trainees had Christian names. That worked out well until it came to Veneranda. We could find no saint of that name, so Cuca suggested that she choose for her special day any day of the year she wanted. But Veneranda was not consoled. She felt that somehow she had been deprived of her day.

The next time I wrote to the Father I told him about this. To my great surprise, an express letter arrived from Rome a short time later, saying that the Father had asked Don Alvaro to check in the Vatican records for a Saint Veneranda, and that Don Alvaro had found one—she was martyred in France, and her feast day was November 14. When I told Veneranda, she jumped for joy—not only did she have a saint's day, but the Father himself had had it found for her! Many years later, when she brought her daughter for the catering course, Veneranda told Cuca with tears in her eyes, "Every year we celebrate November 14 in my family because it is my feast day and Blessed Josemaría found it for me."

Meanwhile, life went on at Invergara House, with classes during the day and other activities for ladies and girls in the evenings and on weekends.

Marlene was the youngest of us, and she was very lively, feminine, and careful about her figure, so when she began to lose weight, I connected it with all that and didn't attach too much importance to it. I also noticed that she began to return very tired from the outings to town, but I attributed that to the hot sun. Then she developed dark circles under her eyes and a dry cough. Tere, who shared a room with her, would sometimes tease her at breakfast, saying, "How's your TB?"

One evening Marlene went to our house at Strathmore for dinner, and Cuca called me. "I'm very concerned about Marlene," she said. "Why don't you take her temperature when she gets home? She's coughing and doesn't look well at all." That gave me a fright. Suddenly all the things I had been noticing came together and looked menacing. As soon as Marlene came in we took her temperature and found that she had a fever. I took her to our doctor, Dr. Ian Batey, the next morning, and after carefully examining her he drew me aside and said solemnly, "This looks very serious." Then, while she was getting ready behind the curtain, he made several calls and sent us out to get chest X rays. In the car I tried to reassure her, but that "very serious" rang in my ears and I found it hard to think straight.

That very evening I got a call from Dr. Batey. Without preliminaries he told me, "Marlene has tuberculosis." "What?" I gasped, thunderstruck. "Yes, she has a large cavity in the lung." He gave me instructions on isolating her, raising the foot of the bed, and taking every precaution to avoid contagion, and then said, "I'm arranging for her immediate admission to the Infectious Diseases Hospital."

Marlene . . . Tuberculosis . . . People died of tuberculosis! How could we let her go to an infectious diseases hospital in Africa? "Can't we send her back to Portugal?" I pleaded. "No," Dr. Batey said with finality. "No airline would agree to carry a person in her condition, and anyway her health wouldn't stand up to it. Do you know where the IDH is?" I did. Mary had worked there for some time. "Then take Marlene there tomorrow afternoon. I'll make all the arrangements."

I hung up the phone and stood there for a few moments, stunned. Then I went in search of Tere, who was giving a hand in the kitchen. "Come for a moment," I said, my voice shaking. "Let's go outside, I have something to tell you and I don't want to alarm the others." The color drained from Tere's face. We went out to the garden in the semidarkness and sat down on the ground under a tree, and I told her all that the doctor had said, and we both cried. Tere kept lamenting, "She's only twenty-one! And I made that awful joke!"

We followed the doctor's instructions and made up Marlene's bed in the front parlor. She lay there pale, inert, and frightened. Though her English was excellent, she kept lapsing into Portuguese. "My mother died of tuberculosis. . . . Am I going to die?" We all hovered around her bed, and Tere, trying to hide her concern, jollied her along, cracking jokes and generally making light of the situation, until she grew more at peace and managed a wan smile.

The next day Tere and I brought Marlene to the Infectious Diseases Hospital. It consisted of three long pavilions, one for each race, quite far apart. Marlene was admitted to the European one, which was the farthest from everything else. It had a gray cement floor and was open on one side to the vast, unbroken expanse of savanna stretching out to the horizon, while on the other a row of doors led to private rooms. There seemed to be no one around, and the place looked really depressing. We were so shattered that when the doctor on duty showed up, he looked at each of us in turn and then asked, "Which one is the patient?"

A kindly English nurse named Margaret was in charge of that pavilion, and she became very fond of Marlene. We were allowed to fix up the room next to hers as a sitting room where, when she was a little better, she could spend the day. We visited her morning and afternoon, and the priest brought her Holy Communion every day.

As soon as the Father learned what had happened, he wrote a long letter telling us he was praying hard for Marlene's health through the intercession of Montserrat Grases, a young woman of Opus Dei who had died in a holy manner two years before, at the age of seventeen. He also told us that he was sending us a reinforcement of two more women from Spain. That was how, in May 1961, Conchita Kaibel and Mila Santurino came to Kenya.

Marlene stayed in that hospital for nearly five months. Fortunately, Tere's acquaintance from the boat, Dr. Ang'awa, was a lung specialist and the one in charge of Marlene. He was able to get her the latest medications, and eventually she got well and returned to Portugal. But Tere and I never quite got over the shock. I blamed myself for not having paid attention to the symptoms and taken Marlene to the doctor earlier, and it made me much more attentive to such warnings.

* 12 *

Kianda College

June was approaching, and with it the expiration of our lease on Invergara House. Kianda wouldn't be ready till September, so we needed another place to live for the three months in between.

One day Tere stumbled on an interesting item in the paper. "Listen to this!" she said. " 'Expatriate going on home leave wants reliable tenant for three months. Fully furnished house, nominal rent.' That's just what we need! Let's apply."

We did. It turned out to be a large three-story house off Ngong Road, with a garden and beyond it wide open spaces leading to the railway track. The offer was incredibly good, so we agreed to caretake the house. When the time came, the seven of us packed up all our belongings and left Invergara, after informing our students of the new location on Churchill Avenue where classes would resume in September.

But by the time we moved into that house, the year's adventures had taken their toll on me. The day after we arrived we started a three-week break for study and rest, but after the first day I fell into a strange condition that reminded me of the illness my mother had had after the death of my baby brother, Gerard . . .

Now it was I who felt nervous and disoriented. Tere brought me to see Dr. Batey, who, taking stock of the situation, promptly declared, "You need an immediate change of environment. Europeans have to get away from the high altitude of Nairobi from time to time. You need to go down to the coast for a good three weeks." He then told us the best way of going about it. Tere eagerly took down his instructions. I sat listening, agape.

"You can drive down—that way you'll see something of the country," he said. "I suggest you go via Moshi, in Tanganyika, where you can spend the night. It's just at the foot of Mount Kilimanjaro, and you'll see plenty of game along that route."

It seemed an enormous venture, and without Tere I wouldn't have dared undertake it. She, Mary, and I set out a couple of days later, from Mary's house at Strathmore. "How lucky you are to be going on safari!" exclaimed Cuca enviously, as she waved us off.

Once we left Nairobi, the road narrowed and became corrugated red marram soil. The car raised big clouds of dust as Mary, wearing her American driving gloves, maneuvered it along the wheel tracks, trying to avoid the hump in the middle.

After several hours Tere called out, "Let's stop for a drink—you must be thirsty, I certainly am!" and reached for the basket of provisions. Mary pulled up under the scanty shade of a thorn tree, and we got out and stretched our legs.

"Listen to the silence," Mary said in a hushed voice. Only the sound of crickets and the occasional cry of a bird broke the midday quiet that hung over the savanna, which stretched as far as the eye could see, shimmering in the heat. "There's no one for miles around," observed Tere. "I wouldn't like to be stuck here."

By the time we reached Moshi, late in the afternoon, the landscape had changed dramatically. The little town at the foot of Mount Kilimanjaro was surrounded by forest, lush vegetation, and flowing streams. But we couldn't see the mountain, as it was shrouded in clouds.

We spent the night at the Kibo Hotel, where Tere and Mary helped me get through a meal in the dining room. The next day was Sunday, and on our way out to Mass we met in the hall a group of tired but jubilant mountaineers. They had just come down from a three-day climb on Kilimanjaro. Their hats were decorated with the dry pink and white flowers that grow on the peak.

We walked along an earthen path, under the shade of luxuriant trees, to the mission church. People in brightly colored garments emerged from little tracks between thick banana plants and joined us, shyly smiling and greeting us in Swahili—"Jambo, habari gani?" (Hello, how are you?). We replied, "Nzuri, na wewe je?" (Very well, and you?).

The church had rough benches fixed to a cement floor and was packed. The Mass was in Swahili, which the Irish priest spoke fluently, and the whole congregation joined in the singing, which was led by a group of men with drums and with bamboo shakers, filled with dried seeds, which they raised and lowered swinging their arms to the beat. It made an attractive swishing sound. With sweet, clear voices and in perfect harmony, the people sang, "Pokea, Baba, zawadi . . ." Tere nudged me and whispered, " 'Baba' is Father. They're saying, 'Bring your gifts to the Father.' " I nodded. At the end of Mass everyone joined in a hymn to "Maryamu Bikira, Mama wa Mungu" (Virgin Mary, Mother of God).

From Moshi we resumed our travel along the Nairobi-Mombasa road, passing by Tsavo, the home of elephants. We looked eagerly out the windows to catch a glimpse of an elephant and were finally rewarded. "There! There!" said Mary, pointing. "Where? Where?" Tere replied, in what became a standard joke. "Don't you see the brown humps near those rocks?" They were small elephants, different from the "Jumbo" type I had expected, but elephants nonetheless, in full view from the road. We also saw zebras and an occasional giraffe. Tere loved the giraffes. "They're so coquettish," she said, "with their long eyelashes!"

Late in the afternoon we arrived at the Kikambala, a seaside hotel recommended by Dr. Batey. In a little whitewashed cottage surrounded by palm trees we hastily unpacked our bags, and then headed for the sea.

"Imagine, all this just for us!" exclaimed Mary. There was no one on the beach except us. Every time a wave retreated, hundreds of little white crabs emerged and scurried in all directions with their awkward gait. Tere gleefully chased them, while Mary and I watched the gold, pink, violet, and indigo sky gradually deepen and the stars come out, first one by one and then in clusters, until the whole night sky seemed to glitter with diamonds. "Where is the Southern Cross?" I asked, remembering romantic stories of sailors using it as a guide. No one knew, but later we learned to identify it.

After two weeks of sunshine and swimming, Tere returned to Nairobi, impatient to see how the construction work at Kianda was coming along, and Margaret Curran came down instead. We moved from the seaside hotel to an apartment lent us by her friend Anne King, in the Tudor area of Mombasa. At the end of the three weeks, I was feeling better and eager to go home.

"Home" was the rented house on Ngong Road that we were to live in for another six weeks before moving to Kianda. It was then that we discovered why one paid so little to caretake a house. I returned from Mombasa refreshed and relaxed. On the first night, with a peaceful sense of security, I left my bedroom window wide open (since my room was on the second floor) and went to sleep.

In the middle of the night I was awakened by a noise near the bedroom door. Thinking I was wanted, I called out, "What is it?" A tense silence was followed by heavy breathing, and then someone jumped onto my bed and out the window! Terrified, I tried to scream, but found my throat was paralyzed. No sound came out. Finally I managed a hoarse "Conchita! Conchita!" In no time the light was on and everyone was in the room, surrounding me anxiously. "What happened?" asked Conchita. I looked around, dazed, and suddenly realized that my purse was gone. A thief!

We informed the police, but they couldn't do much. Thieves kept coming, so we took our own precautions, such as collecting the "bombs"—enormous bullet-shaped doorstops—to arm ourselves with at night. Very early one morning Conchita was looking out an upstairs window when two hands suddenly appeared on the sill. She banged on it with a bomb and immediately they disappeared, with ladder and all.

One night thieves came in downstairs. We heard nothing. It was only the following morning that we found a window broken and pictures and other items strewn about the garden. "How strange," said Tere. "They didn't take anything, not even the silver, and there's plenty of it. They must have been looking for something specific." "Maybe the owners keep guns," speculated Margaret. "A lot of people do." We never found out what the thieves were after, but they didn't come again.

In September we moved into our new Kianda. With its cream-colored stone walls, red-painted window frames, red corrugated iron roof, and surrounding flowers and shrubs, it had a fairy-tale charm. The rains were about to come and the morning sky was overcast, so that the lilac, bell-shaped flowers of the big jacaranda tree in front of the bungalow contrasted with the heavy gray clouds. I liked to stand beneath that tall tree, beneath its outspread branches, listening to the gentle plop-plop of the flowers as they formed a carpet at my feet. The crisp cool air was hushed and somehow reminded me of snow falling.

Although we had been able to admit several Asian students, only twelve of the original seventeen European girls were coming back to Kianda. After the first term the other five had transferred to a college in town. That was a blow. We still had to prove ourselves in the London Pitman exams, in December, and this show of no confidence unsettled both Tere and me. However, it made us all the more determined to do well.

The term got off to a good start, with a full quota of students. Tere soon perfected her typing classes, beating out the rhythm with a wooden hammer and occasionally chastising a naughty student with a sharp "Go out to the garden and count the flowers!"

I gave the language classes in the tiny all-purpose room, in full view of the garden, where the sunlight was so intense that it dimmed the bright colors of the bougainvillea and the jade green of the jacaranda leaves. Iridescent blue and yellow hummingbirds flew from flower to flower dipping their curved beaks in search of nectar, and weaverbirds circled about with bits of grass and straw in their beaks, busily building their nests, which hung downwards in clusters from the trees. While the girls were writing, I occasionally looked out the window, fascinated by the splash of color and all the activity going on outside—such a contrast to the monotonous city roofs I had seen from the classroom windows of my childhood.

It wasn't until the following year that the first African student came to Kianda. One day Mrs. Gecaga called me and said, "I think I have found a girl for Kianda, and I'd like you to meet her. She's the daughter of a good friend of mine." We agreed to meet at her office in town the next day.

When I arrived there, a girl of around eighteen was sitting on the bench outside, wearing a simple dress and clutching a plastic purse to her knees. She didn't look up at me. Mrs. Gecaga came out, smiling, and invited us both in. "This is Evelyn Karungari," she said. "She wants to take the secretarial courses at Kianda, don't you, Evelyn?" The girl nodded, looking very serious, almost stern.

"Evelyn is the second of nine children," Mrs. Gecaga said, "and it would make her father very happy if she could study at Kianda. Evelyn's father is a forward-looking man. He speaks English at home with his children because he wants them to be able to communicate with foreigners. I think you will find she is capable, and North Carolina College in the United States is willing to sponsor her."

I explained that it would not be easy for Evelyn, as the other girls were Europeans and Asians who had finished high school and in most cases had English as their first language. From Evelyn's determined little face and raised chin, however, it was clear that she was ready to take on the challenge. And she did.

Evelyn spent two years at Kianda. At that time Jack Block's daughters Lyn and Liz were there, and so were Julie Manji, Aruna Shah, and other girls from prominent Kenyan families. Many arrived in chauffeur-driven cars and took the courses easily in stride. For Evelyn it was an intense struggle.

After school hours Margaret taught her Gregg Shorthand, which is less complicated than Pitman, and she spent more time at the typewriter and improving her English. But though she was the only African in the school, Evelyn mixed like one more and was accepted by all. Shortly after the term began, Doria Block called me and said, "I want to tell you that my two girls are very happy. They have made friends with an African girl, and I'm pleased, because that way they'll learn not to stick to their own little group."

None of the other students knew what it cost Evelyn to be one more. She faced many privations but determinedly overcame them. She studied hard in school, and at night, by the light of a hurricane lamp, read magazines her father brought her.

We invited Evelyn's parents for tea and showed them around the school. Evelyn demonstrated her typing for them and took down some dictation in shorthand and read it back, while they beamed with pride. She had grown in confidence and now had a ready smile.

When Evelyn finished Kianda's secretarial program, Margaret took her to the interview at the end of which she became the first African secretary employed by the East African Common Services.

Meanwhile, Tom Mboya hadn't forgotten our school. When his fiancée, Pamela Odede, returned with a degree from Western College for Women (in Ohio), he sent her there to learn about home management and Western-style cooking.

At that time Margaret was running a Continental Cooking course for ladies, so Pamela joined them. A tall, slim Luo girl of about my own age, she had a charming smile and manner, but was a bit overwhelmed by the prospect of her imminent marriage because Tom was already a prominent public figure and was a staunch Catholic, whereas she was an Anglican. They were to be married in the Catholic Church and she wanted to know the faith better. I gave her some classes, and she in fact became a Catholic shortly before their wedding.

Pamela put Margaret's lessons into practice in the entertaining she had to do on account of Tom's position. "The governor, Sir Patrick Renison, is coming to our house for tea next week," she announced one day. "What do you think I should prepare?" Margaret gave her some suggestions, and when the tea was over Pamela called to say that everything had gone very well. I wasn't surprised, because besides being a charming hostess, Pamela had a strong practical sense.

We became good friends, and I followed the progress of her first pregnancy and the birth of the baby, whom they named Maureen. I often visited the Mboya home, and would look in on the baby as she stood peering over the white bars of her crib, tiny hands clutching the crossbar, her round, serious little face crowned with *matutas* (clumps of short braids).

Maureen was followed by twins, Peter and Patrick. Patrick had sickle-cell anemia. His parents did everything they could, taking him to doctors in Kenya and overseas, but there was no cure. Often he suffered severe attacks of pain which drove his mother to distraction. Shortly before the twins' third birthday Patrick had to be hospitalized, and a few days later Pamela called to tell me that he had died.

I went right away to her home. Pamela had just returned from the hospital and was sitting disconsolate on the bed with the little bundle beside her. I sat next to her, and she asked wistfully, "Would you like to see him? He just looks asleep." Later on there was a funeral service at the house. Patrick lay in a coffin lined with yellow satin, his toys around him, and while the priest talked, I found it difficult not to imagine that the yellow coverlet was rising and falling with the child's breathing.

Life went on, and Pamela had another child, whom she named Susan. At first she was very much afraid that this child too might have the disease, which is hereditary, but she didn't. Susan was a graceful little girl on whom the cares of life seemed to weigh less heavily than on Maureen. She was affectionate and expressive. I have a vivid memory of driving up to their gate, beeping the horn to have it opened, and a little figure dressed in a pink woolen frock running out waving her arms and crying, "Aunty Olga's here! Aunty Olga's here!"

Sometimes Tom arrived home while I was visiting. He was an extraordinary man, with a real charisma. I never failed to be impressed by his presence, which filled the room when he entered. Invariably he asked me with a smile, "How's the school?" Generally Tom headed straight for his study, but occasionally he stayed for a while chatting with Pamela and me about the children or the latest developments in his work or at Kianda. Occasionally he talked about his experiences of racial discrimination during the colonial times.

"Once, when one of my European colleagues at the Sanitation Department was away on leave," he told us,

"I was over there testing milk samples, and a European lady came in with one. She looked around for a few moments and didn't say anything. I said, 'Good morning, madam,' and she turned and asked, as if looking right through me, 'Isn't there anybody here?' Another time the inspector asked me to show a European lady to the office she was looking for, and as I moved towards the lift she exclaimed angrily, 'Do you expect me to get into a lift with that *boy*?'"

I remembered the Father's teachings that we are all equal and that the Africans deserve to be treated marvelously well, and was eager to make up for such indignities.

13

Uhuru!

In the early fifties the struggle for independence that was sweeping across Africa reached Kenya with a particularly bloody struggle by the Mau Mau against the British settlers. Many of the Mau Mau had learned the skills of war in distant places, such as Burma, where they were conscripted by the British during World War II.

In 1952 the British colonial government declared a state of emergency, and in 1953 they put Jomo Kenyatta, who was perceived as a particular threat, into jail. With him went several other freedom fighters: Bildad Kaggia, Achieng Oneko, Paul Ngei . . . This move only served to unify the whole country behind Kenyatta, giving rise to a great clamor for his release. But the release would not take place until after the 1961 general elections. In 1953 the governor, Patrick Renison, was calling Kenyatta "a leader unto darkness and death."

What sort of person was Kenyatta? Why did he arouse such emotions?

A thickset man with penetrating eyes, pronounced forehead, and rugged features, he had an aura of power about him that could be intimidating. He was an undoubted leader, with a magnetic personality. The people revered him and called him "Baba Taifa" (Father of the Nation) or "Mzee" (the Old Man, or Elder).

Mrs. Gecaga came to see us shortly before his release in August 1961. "I don't think there will be any trouble," she said, "but if there is, all of you are to come to my house." However, everything went peacefully.

In January 1962 Kenyatta was elected to the Legislative Council as member for Fort Hall (Murang'a) when the incumbent stepped down for him. Immediately he began preaching reconciliation between races and ethnic groups. Kenyatta proved himself to be not a leader unto darkness and death, but rather the father and symbol of nationhood.

Kenya attained internal self-government on June 1, 1963, under a Kenya African National Union (KANU) government, with Kenyatta as Prime Minister and Tom Mboya as Minister of Justice and Constitutional Affairs. The date for full independence was set for December 12, 1963.

The atmosphere was euphoric as people prepared to celebrate their longed-for freedom, and although Kenyatta called for "uhuru na kazi" (freedom and work), not everyone understood this. We heard, for example, that Africans were being sold pictures of European-owned houses and cars "for you after independence." It was a bit alarming. We could only pray that with time people would realize that the only way to build a strong nation is by hard work.

Because of all these things there was a certain amount of insecurity in the air. One afternoon in early December the Counsellor called to say, "The Father wants you to move as soon as possible to the women's house at Strathmore. He is concerned about the vulnerability of your bungalow, which is very near the reserve. You'd better move tonight." The women's house at Strathmore was part of a vast three-story stone building that constituted a veritable fortress.

I immediately alerted Tere and then called Cuca, saying, "The Father wants all of us to move to your house, and we're coming tonight." "All of you? Why?" cried Cuca, amazed. We packed up our household goods and personal belongings and ferried them to Strathmore, and then locked up all the classrooms. Late in the evening we arrived to an exuberant welcome and cheerfully installed ourselves in the single rooms, each of which now had to hold three people.

We went to Kianda every morning after breakfast and returned in the evening, leaving everything locked up and a watchman on the compound. One morning, while we were still at breakfast, an urgent message came from Absalom, the watchman. Thieves had broken into Kianda during the night! We hastily got into the car and sped towards Kianda, wondering how this could have happened, since there were bars on all the windows.

When we got to the house, we found Absalom waiting, but could see nothing amiss. Then he brought us to the back and pointed at two gaping holes in the windows. The bars had been severed and forced back, leaving room enough to pass the typewriters through. All eight were gone! Absalom looked sheepish; he had heard nothing.

The typewriters were the mainstay of the secretarial program and would be expensive to replace. "Of course you had them insured?" Agnes Lavelle said, raising her eyebrows, when I told her what had happened. No, we hadn't, but we learned our lesson.

In addition to replacing the bars, we had wooden shutters installed on the inside of the windows of the typing room as an extra precaution, and Mr. Singh, the contractor, converted the shower room into a strong room with shelves and steel door. Every evening after school Tere and I went through the ceremony of putting the typewriters on carts and transferring them to the shelves of the strong room, which we then locked, and every morning we carried out the same procedure in reverse. No more typewriters were stolen.

As December 12 approached, the air of jubilation which had caught hold of the whole country gathered momentum. Jomo Kenyatta was in the lead, supervising preparations and encouraging everyone. "Don't flag in your efforts to build the country," he kept saying. "Work to create a new nation with one soul, without difference of race, tribe, class, culture, or language. *Harambee!* [All together!]"

It was exciting to assist at the birth of a nation. Every day brought something new. "Today there's a special edition—sixty-four pages!" Carlota announced one day, waving the newspaper. "It has the design for the national flag." Then she read: "President Kenyatta personally designed the colours of the flag long before Kenyans knew they would be independent. He designed it to have meaning for the whole of Africa, with black to signify the people of Africa, green the fertile land which gives them sustenance, and red for the blood which African freedom fighters shed in order to free Mother Africa from colonial bondage."

Conchita copied out the words of the national anthem and escaped to the living room whenever she could to play the record, paper in hand, and learn it. "Listen," she said, catching hold of my skirt as I passed by, and she read the lyrics:

> O God of all creation,
> Bless this our land and nation.
> Justice be our shield and defender.
> May we dwell in unity,
> Peace, and liberty.
> Plenty be found within our borders.
> Let one and all arise,
> With hearts both strong and true.
> Service be our earnest endeavour,
> And our homeland of Kenya,
> Heritage of splendour,
> Firm may we stand to defend.
> Let all with one accord,
> In common bond united,
> Build this our nation together,
> And the glory of Kenya,
> The fruit of our labour,
> Fill every heart with thanksgiving.

"Isn't it beautiful?" she said. "The Kenyans are God-fearing people. God must love them very much, because it hasn't stopped raining all these days, and for them rain is a sign of his blessing. But I hope it stops for the celebrations on the twelfth. The Duke of Edinburgh is coming, and there will be three days of festivities. The town is full of flags and bunting and big arches over the road with 'UHURU' [freedom] written on them."

On December 11 Jomo Kenyatta went to the airport to meet the Duke of Edinburgh. He wore on his lapel the KANU emblem: a cock, which heralds the break of day. The Duke went up to examine it, and Kenyatta, smiling broadly, took the emblem off and pinned it on his jacket.

"Midnight—and up goes the flag. KENYA FREE! A vast crowd at Nairobi's Independence Arena last night roared a welcome to the newest nation of Africa. Kenya joined the councils of the world at one minute past midnight, as the green, red, black, and white standard broke where a few minutes before, the Union Jack had flown," said the December 12 edition of the *Daily Nation*. In our living room at Strathmore everyone sat glued to the black-and-white television set. "The lights dimmed suddenly at midnight in the arena," we heard. "Then two officers lowered the Union Jack, in total darkness. A moment later the lights blazed on again, and the Kenya flag was slowly raised in its place."

At that moment Encarnación produced a large Kenyan flag she had made and held it over the set and we all cheered. We watched as the army band, out in full regalia with colobus monkey helmets and shining brass instruments, played the national anthem and fireworks exploded in the sky and people shed tears full of emotion. "Conchita, you're crying!" Mary exclaimed. "Of course!" retorted Conchita, unabashed.

Mrs. Gecaga had given us invitations to the next day's garden party at the state capitol. There I was able to greet President Kenyatta and his wife, Mama Ngina. I was impressed by the shrewd look in his eyes that seemed to pierce you through. He was unquestionably a great statesman. In the fifteen years that Kenyatta was president, Kenya developed by leaps and bounds, attained a certain degree of national unity, and became an oasis of peace in the region.

Repeating the slogan "Harambee!"—a slogan forever to be associated with the father of the nation—Kenyatta invited all non-Africans who were willing to cooperate with the new government to stay on in Kenya and work hand in hand to build our country.

Two decades after his death, Jomo Kenyatta still presents a formidable figure to historians and other observers. Kristina Kenyatta, once a student at Kianda College, provided some interesting insights in a taped conversation which I have her permission to quote. "My mother," she says, "had gone to him in Lodwar a little earlier, and we joined them later. . . . I was only seven. When we got there we had to be introduced. Of course I didn't know which of the five gentlemen was my father, because he had been in detention since I was six months old. What sticks in my mind is the way that he tried, under very difficult circumstances, to make up for lost time, even though we had no financial means whatsoever. He taught us tasks that would normally be taught only to boys. He had no discrimination. He wanted his daughters and sons to be equally prepared for life. The other thing was education. He spent a great deal of time reading to us. He was particularly concerned that we be articulate, especially in the English language. . . . Regardless of his busy schedule, Kenya still being a young nation, he spent a lot of time with his family."

Kenyatta was apparently a very spiritual man. "He was an early riser," says Kristina. "He would wake up at around five in the morning, climb up to the room at the top of the house, which had a magnificent view of Mount Kenya, and spend time there alone. . . . He used that time for meditation. He never wanted to be linked to any one religion or church, as he felt keenly that he represented everyone's aspirations, as he was the father of the nation."

And what a nation!

Kenya is a beautiful country with an amazing variety of landscapes. Its huge expanses of savanna country are home to some of the most impressive game in the world: lions, leopards, cheetahs, elephants, giraffes, and all kinds of antelopes. The bird life is also impressive. The flamingos at Lake Nakuru are an incredible feast for the eyes. The Great Rift Valley splits Kenya in two, and its escarpments and the hills and lakes that dot its floor have to be seen to be believed.

For me, though, the most important thing has been the people, among whom I have, over the years, made deep and lasting friendships. Kenya is made up of over forty tribal groupings whose cultures, traditions, and religions are as diverse and rich as the people themselves.

Over the years, Africans have learned to value education. A teacher—*mwalimu*—is highly respected. President Julius Nyerere of neighboring Tanzania, for example, prided himself on being a teacher and was known as Mwalimu Nyerere. Those of us who came to the country to help in education were therefore well placed to help bring about a real change in the lives of a wide cross section of the people. The spirit of Opus Dei, Christianity lived out in the ordinary circumstances of daily life and work, was admirably suited to Kenyatta's calls for *uhuru na kazi* and *harambee*.

The career school at Strathmore had itself become a kind of harambee, with thirty trainees from different tribes. Florence Auma, Frida Mudimo, and Priscilla Nekesa were Luhyas from around Lake Victoria; Mary Nduku, Mary Mumbua, and Anastasia Katiti, Kambas;

and Roselida Atieno and Margaret Akinyi, Luos from the province of Nyanza. At first they were all a little apprehensive about living and working with girls from tribes they had only heard about and sometimes as enemies. But they soon forgot their differences, mixing freely and even learning one another's songs and dances.

As it was not yet common to see people of different races and tribes associating with one another, the girls often attracted the attention of passersby on their outings to town. Occasionally someone was overheard to comment knowingly, "They are from Strathmore!" One day Willimena Indakuli, a Luhya, was talking and laughing animatedly with another trainee, and she ran into a friend who stopped them, drew her aside, and asked in a shocked voice, "How can you be laughing so much with that Kamba girl?"

Outings in the van always ended on the same jolly note. As soon as the gray stone building of Strathmore came into sight, everyone began to sing:

> Home again, home again,
> I am going to see my home again,
> I am going to see me dear home.
> I never forget my home.
> Cuca is there,
> Mila is there,
> Florence is there . . .

The song continued until all who had remained behind were named or the vehicle came to a standstill.

Florence Auma was brought over from Luhya land by her uncle. A little distant at first, she soon thawed out and became part and parcel of the household. "At first I didn't like the training because I thought it was too much hard work," she once told Cuca, with a shy smile. "But then I learned about Opus Dei and that work can be offered and made holy. I'll always remember this place. Africans love each other very much because we're all Africans, but I thought Europeans didn't like us. It's different here. You love us even more than we love ourselves. I've seen it."

Christmas drew near, and with it holiday time for the trainees, although the work in the house would continue as usual. "When are you going home for the holidays?" Tere asked Florence Auma and Mary Mumbua. "Are you going home?" was the reply. "No," Tere answered, taken aback. "Well, then, neither are we," Florence said with finality.

On January 6, 1963, Florence and Mary became the first African women to ask admission to Opus Dei. The little seed just planted was already bearing fruit. The Father was overjoyed. He got the news on his birthday, January 9, and said it was the best birthday present he could have received.

When the first trainees finished their training, we helped them find employment as assistant caterers in schools and hospitals up-country. In Nairobi these jobs were still given only to men. But it was a breakthrough, and the success of the girls was very encouraging. One was promoted to supervisor in her school. They kept in touch and occasionally telephoned to ask our advice, saying, for instance, "There is a board meeting next week and they have asked for refreshments. What do you think I should prepare?"

From the Strathmore training emerged the Kibondeni School of Institutional Management, the first institution of its kind in Kenya.

I invited Pamela Mboya to visit Kibondeni, and she was very impressed. Afterwards she said, "We must meet more often. I can't get over the way in which you are all trying to help. I want to know why you do it."

She asked me a lot of questions that day: "Don't you mind having left your own country to come to ours that is just getting started, with all its difficulties?" "Do you expect to get many people to join you?" "What will you do when there are plenty of Africans in Opus Dei?" And then she said, "I would be very sorry if you left, because you really belong here. You have helped lay the foundations." I told her that I loved the country and had every intention of staying. I meant it with all my heart.

✷ 14 ✷

Uhuru Is Also for Women

Kenya was very much a man's country, although I realized that in their quiet, unassuming way, women were the backbone of African society. Their silent hard work, patience, stamina, and concern to hold the family together through thick and thin at whatever cost to themselves, I found heroic. Yet generally women were not esteemed by men and their sacrifices were taken for granted—except in the case of the men's mothers.

I first noticed this exception when Mrs. Jemimah Gecaga brought me to visit her brother Dr. Njoroge Mungai. He lived in an elegant suburban house, and his mother had come to stay with him for a while. She was a simple, illiterate Kikuyu woman from the countryside, but her son treated her with great respect and deference and she was clearly the center of the household. Her weather-beaten face and worn, cracked hands attested to a life of toil, but her motherly heart was still giving.

"Men respect their mothers very much, don't they?" I said to Mrs. Gecaga afterwards.

"Yes," she replied. "Usually it is the mother who brings up the children, and she educates them with what she sells from the shamba. But men must learn to respect their wives also, and this can only happen when women are free, no longer subservient to men. So far freedom has been for men, but *uhuru* is also for women. Our women need education, because what good is freedom if ignorance and poverty still bind them?"

The issue of education kept coming up again and again. Kenyatta, for example, according to Kristina, treated his daughters as if they were boys, preparing them for life in the same way. And Tom Mboya, in his book *Freedom and After* (London: Andre Deutsch, 1963), expresses a lot of concern for the education of women. He says (on page 142), "The really depressing part of studying the school 'pyramid' in Kenya—or anywhere in Africa—comes when you see the numbers who have to drop out after four and eight and twelve years because there are not the schools, still less the teachers, to take them through the next stage."

Regarding women's education specifically, he says: "We should concern ourselves with the role women can play in the preparation for independence. They have a part to fill in education, in agricultural development, in business, in the taking over of the civil service, in the trade unions, in the political parties, where they can especially generate the spirit of challenge. I see the role of the African woman, not only in terms of her own individual challenge in the task of creating an enlightened family and community, particularly in rural areas, where many men have left to move to the towns; she has also the job of taking part like any other citizen in the overall development of the country" (page 160).

The civil service included secretaries, but Kianda still had few African students, even though after Kenya's gaining of independence the colonial civil servants had left and both government and business offices were threatened with collapse due to a shortage of personnel. The handful of Africans trained at Kianda suddenly found themselves in great demand and were quickly promoted to positions of responsibility as personal secretaries. However, this was only a drop in the ocean.

"African secretaries are needed, we can train them, but they can't afford to come—that sums it up," I said one day when Tere, Cuca, and I sat studying the situation of Kianda College. Cuca had joined the Kianda staff when Margaret became ill and had to return to England.

"Some parents could afford it if they really wanted," observed Tere, "but how do you convince a peasant farmer to pay tuition for his daughter to train as a secretary and afterwards work in an office with men? It goes against all the traditions. Girls are not supposed to be seen in the company of men until they get married."

"It's a vicious circle, isn't it?" I said. "Education for freedom, freedom for education . . ." And I recalled my conversation with Jemimah Gecaga.

"Evelyn Karungari was sponsored by North Carolina College. Maybe we could get more sponsors like that," said Cuca.

"Yes, but we're talking about almost every African who applies to Kianda," I answered. "How can we hope to get sponsors for all of them?"

Not long after that, Tere found a training program advertised in the newspaper by the East African Railways and Harbours Corporation. "They are offering," she said, "to pay for the training of technical personnel on condition that they afterwards work for this company for a time. Don't you think Kianda could get in on such a program?" It seemed a very good idea.

We went to see EAR&H's general manager, Mr. Hobson, and he agreed that it was important to include secretaries in the training program and offered ten places on the spot. The terms were incredibly good. EAR&H would provide tuition, room and board, and even pocket money, and the students were assured of employment at the end of the training. "I would only ask," he said, "that you carry out the preliminary selection yourselves and send us the best candidates for shortlisting. Keep in mind that we are an East African corporation and therefore want to recruit staff as far afield as possible."

"That means we'll have to visit schools in different parts of the country and explain about the course of study at Kianda!" Cuca said later, looking delighted at the prospect. "It makes all the difference that it will be paid for and the girls even given some pocket money. We can explain to their fathers what a respectable career it is and that their daughters will be safe with us . . ." Then she stopped abruptly and asked, "Where will the girls live? That's the first thing they'll want to know."

I thought of some half-empty residence halls at the Royal Technical College, where I had taught for a while, and said, "Let me talk to Miss Janisch, the dorm supervisor. Maybe she can let us rent a floor in one of the women's halls."

Miss Janisch was quite amenable. She agreed to let us use one floor of Hall B, provided that someone on the Kianda staff occupied the assistant supervisor's apartment and took responsibility for the care and discipline of the students.

Circumstances combined to provide that person. Ever since the school began, we had almost constantly been dogged by the problem of the shorthand teacher. Audrey Leitch had left after a couple of years because her husband was transferred to Nigeria, and we never could get a permanent replacement. Every term we agonized over a shorthand teacher and I would fill in until we managed to get one, but it couldn't keep going like that, so we finally decided to ask for a member of the Work from Ireland.

Constance Gillan was a native of the Aran Islands and an associate member of Opus Dei, which is one who shares the same vocation as a numerary member except for being more conditioned by family or professional ties. Constance readily agreed to come, although she was a degreed teacher, in her late forties, and not a secretary. In order to be able to help us out she had to spend a year in Dublin studying Pitman Shorthand and working for the Shorthand Teacher's Diploma, as well as learn to drive. When she came to Kenya she could live in the assistant supervisor's apartment and look after the students.

"How will we get the girls to and from Kianda?" I

asked Cuca. "Public transportation is unreliable and we're six miles out of town."

"I've been thinking about that," she said. "We need to get a minibus, and I know of one for sale. The problem will be to get a good driver."

We bought the van, and Cuca went to the Employment Bureau in search of a driver, and there she discovered Cefa Ndeda, from western Kenya. Soon he was as much a part of Kianda as anyone on the staff. He drove the navy blue van as if Kianda's honor was at stake, priding himself on keeping it free of so much as a single scratch. The students called him "Speedy" because he was so slow and careful.

Like all Kenyan men, Ndeda was always avid for news. The day he heard on the radio the news about the first man walking on the moon, he was indignant. "They went all the way to the moon," he said, "just to collect *mchanga* [dirt]!"

Tere and Cuca traveled with him to the mission schools on the shores of Lake Victoria in search of students, and they returned after three days, full of stories of their adventures.

"We stood on the equator line!" Cuca crowed. "It's marked by a big board with a map of Africa and the equator running through it. I took some photos. I hope they come out."

"Ndeda, of course, drove very carefully," said Tere, "and he was also our protector. It was very hot, but when we suggested stopping for a while at a place he didn't think suitable, Ndeda refused. 'This is not a safe place,' he said." At this, Cuca beamed.

"They are very hospitable at the missions," Tere went on. "There was always a guesthouse and a place at table for visitors. We explained to the principal of each school about Kianda and the secretarial training that could open up so many opportunities for their girls, as well as the spiritual and cultural education available to them through the work of the college chaplaincy and the contact with students from other races and tribes. They liked the idea very much, seeing it as a continuation of their own work."

We were all impressed by what the missionaries had accomplished. Despite incredible obstacles, they had dauntlessly laid foundations for Christianization, education, and development upon which others, including the new government, could build. Missionaries had been working for over fifty years all over Kenya, bringing Christianity from Mombasa to Nairobi and on to western Kenya. Each mission had its own church, built with the help of the villagers, and also a rectory, a school, and perhaps a dispensary and a convent. All the surrounding villages now boasted flourishing Christian communities.

"What about the girls? Did you talk to them?" I asked Cuca, who looked fit to burst with all she had experienced. It was Tere who answered.

"Yes," she said, "but they interviewed us! After the formal talk in the classroom we stayed on to answer questions, and they didn't stop. 'Is it true that there are *wazungus* studying at Kianda?' 'Where do the students live?' 'Is there a uniform?' I told them there's no uniform because the students are expected to dress as they would in an office; it's part of the training. They were curious about our clothes and hairstyles and accessories, because the only wazungus they're familiar with are the missionaries."

"Did any of them want to apply?"

"Oh yes, I think they'll all apply," Tere said. "Kianda opened up a whole new world for them. After a year's training the girls will earn a salary beyond anything their parents could dream of. The problem is going to be to make the selection."

"We have to take more students! Don't you think we could interest other people in sponsoring girls to

Kianda?" asked Cuca. "What about the mayor of Nairobi? Surely the City Council needs secretaries."

Mr. Charles Rubia was now the mayor of Nairobi. Tere and I made an appointment to see him, and he received us like old friends. When we asked about the possibility of sponsorship for future secretaries, he took to the idea at once. "It will solve a big problem we have, as most of our secretarial staff were expatriates and have left Kenya," he said. "I'll look into it with my council, but I think you can count on sponsorship from us." We thanked him profusely, but he cut us short, saying, "We knew each other when you were nobody and I was nobody."

The Nairobi City Council did join the sponsorship program, and I was asked to sit on the selection panel. It was a grueling experience for the girls. They had come straight from their up-country schools to participate in the interviews, which were held on the first floor of the imposing city hall. They sat waiting on benches in the corridor and were called one by one into the large, wainscoted boardroom. Each girl entered alone and walked across the red-carpeted floor to a chair in front of the huge mahogany table, watched by a row of formidable-looking gentlemen and several ladies, including myself, seated behind it.

Everyone on the panel asked a question or two and made notes on a pad. "Why do you want to take the secretarial training?" "What do you know about the City Council?" "Are you planning to get married soon?" I tried my best to look encouraging and ask easy questions, but the girls perspired and wrung their handkerchiefs in their laps, scarcely daring to raise their eyes.

In April 1965 the mayor and some members of the City Council paid a formal visit to Kianda. To the amusement of the students, Mr. Rubia sat at a typewriter and Cuca gave him an impromptu lesson. Afterwards he gave a short speech, broadcast on radio and television, in which he said, "If Kianda is now at the forefront of teaching institutions dedicated to the education of women, it is because it has worked with all and for all."

The sponsorship program was taken up by many companies and government-affiliated organizations all over East Africa and beyond, and thus hundreds of African girls came to train at Kianda. They learned values that we communicated to them through the spirit of Opus Dei and they made them their own, so that employers commented on the "discipline," for want of a better word, that the Kianda secretaries had acquired. Kianda was turning out polished, competent young women of integrity, and the opportunities open to them constantly increased. The first to benefit were their families, because a secretary in the home meant an immediate rise in the standard of living and possibilities for further education of siblings.

The girls were very sensitive to the needs of their families, and while in training sent most of their pocket money home.

Lucy Karigi, a bright Kikuyu girl with a charming shy smile and soft honey-colored eyes, was sponsored by the Nairobi City Council. I asked her, "What will you do when you leave Kianda and start working? Do you have any plans for the future?" "I only want one thing," she said determinedly. "I want to earn enough money to build my mother a stone house."

Applications poured in, some of them quite unusual. One girl wrote asking for "a seat in your legendary college." Another sought sponsorship because "my father is suffering from financial epilepsy." Other fathers were at the opposite end of the financial ladder. One application arrived with "Father's occupation: Business Tycoon." Kristina Kenyatta's had there, "Father's occupation: President." Cuca carefully preserved a photocopy of a check for Kristina's tuition which was signed in the President's own handwriting, "Jomo Kenyatta."

Kristina studied in the same class as the daughter of our gardener.

Each year the students did well in the Pitman exams and Kianda received a letter of congratulations from the Pitman office in London. However, it took time for the papers to be graded and returned to Kenya, so the students sometimes had to wait for months before they had their certificates and could be employed.

"It's so frustrating for them," complained Cuca. "Couldn't we ask the Ministry of Education to authorize Kianda to issue its own certificates?"

"I think we could try," I said. "After all, Kianda is well known now. I'll make an appointment with the Minister of Education and ask him about it."

The Minister, a middle-aged Kikuyu, received me politely in his office. I had just begun to explain the purpose of my visit when suddenly he sat back and said, "You're an American, aren't you?" "Yes," I replied, surprised. "All Americans have very bad teeth," the Minister said, observing me closely. "Show me yours."

I was sensitive about my teeth. All my life they had given me problems. Now I felt that the Minister was making me share in the humiliations the Africans had so often been put through. I accepted it, and nothing more was said about teeth. I went on to make my request for Kianda certificates. The Minister said he would look into it and we would be informed in due course. The following month the *Kenya Gazette* carried a notice that Kianda Secretarial College was officially authorized to issue its own certificates. Kianda was now an independent college.

"Poles, Italians, Irish, English, Kenyans, Americans, Goans, Kikuyus, Luhyas, Tavetas, Luos, Ismailis, Hindus, Punjabis—what can all these nationalities, tribes, and sects have in common?" began an article on Kianda College published in a Nairobi daily paper. The Father had told us that our school should be multiracial, without any discrimination as to race, religion, or tongue, and now this was a tangible reality.

Parviz Merali and another girl were Ismailis, and during Ramadan, which occurs at what in Africa is the hottest time of the year, they kept a strict fast, eating and drinking nothing all day. "You are offering that for your religion?" I asked. Both girls nodded, and Parviz said, "Catholics also fast, don't they? It's good that we all make sacrifices for God."

One afternoon, while the girls were calculating their speed after a typing test, Tere put her head around the door of my office and said with a big grin, "Do you know what we have just realized? No matter how well you know another language, when it comes to counting, everyone does it in her native tongue. Shobhna is counting in Hindu, Helen Nzuki in Kikuyu, Maitena in French, Pramila in Cathchi, Robinah in Luo, Alicja in Polish, Rose Munubi in Kikamba, Agnes Kwenge in Luganda, Celine in Swahili . . . Out of twenty-three students, only two are counting in English!"

We were always on the lookout for people who could give talks to our students on current affairs and opportunities, and Mrs. Elise Rockart, from Boston, came to give a talk on IBM. She took a lively interest in the school and volunteered to help with the Office Practice classes. Petite, always perfectly groomed, brisk and businesslike, with a ready laugh and a warm heart, she was a welcome addition to our staff. Elise took great trouble over her classes and exacted good work. She was genuinely fond of her students and very much wanted them to do well, and they responded.

Elise never let pass a chance to help her students improve, though her approach could be quite unorthodox. One example was the way she tackled the girls' tendency to remove their shoes in class, kick them aside, and comfortably wiggle their free toes. Elise made no comment, but one day she breezed into the room, carrying her books with her usual air of efficiency and control . . . but barefoot! She sat down, opened a book, and began wiggling her toes. The girls were mesmerized, they kept staring at her feet, until Elise looked up and asked, "What's the matter?" "You have no shoes on!" "What looks better, shoes or no shoes?" "Shoes." No shoes were removed in class again.

Another time Elise entered the classroom with her hair full of pencils (how she managed to fix them in her soft hair, I don't know), again seemingly impervious to the fact. By now the girls knew Elise, and her appearance was enough to send the whole class into fits of laughter . . . and no one stuck pencils in her hair anymore.

Then in 1965 I met Carlette Roeske, at a cocktail party at the Mboyas' home. I saw this tall, blonde lady with a charming smile and went over to greet her. She and her husband, Pim, had just come from Holland, as he was on temporary duty with the Ministry of Finance, and Carlette was quite bored, as she didn't know many people here and had nothing much to do.

I told her about the French classes at Kianda and she showed an interest in teaching French, so I invited her to visit the college. After going around the classrooms and meeting the teachers, Carlette commented, "The atmosphere here shows a lot of dedication." Besides teaching French on a volunteer basis, she also took part in the fundraising activities organized by Opus Dei cooperators and friends: bazaars, family days, coffee parties . . .

When Pim's work was finished, the Roeskes returned to Holland. It was a sad day when we had to say goodbye to Carlette. I little dreamed what help the couple would give us in the future.

The sponsorship program brought us into contact with many people from different walks of life. On the one hand, there were the companies and government organizations that were doing the sponsoring, and on the other, the parents and school principals and priests and nuns who had girls they wanted to bring to Kianda. That was how I met Father Raphael Ndingi, from the Machakos diocese, in the late sixties.

He told me that he was going to Washington, D.C., for further studies, and as my parents were living there then, I gave him their address and wrote to tell them that he might get in touch. He did, and my father invited him to stay with them for several weeks. Mother told me how much she enjoyed the long talks they had about religion, and that she was delighted to find that they shared the same ideas. They built up a lasting relationship, and my parents came to look upon him as a son. Mother painted a portrait of Father Ndingi for his mother, and he told me that it was put up in a prominent place in their family home. Father Ndingi is now the archbishop of Nairobi.

Over the years, Kianda has had a great impact on the lives of very many Kenyan women. This is due not only to their professional formation but also to the deep and lasting friendships that we forged, which enriched us all. This friendship with their teachers enhanced the girls' sense of dignity, of being persons worthy of consideration and respect, capable of mutual exchange in a give-and-take relationship.

* 15 *

Kianda Residence

"Kianda is the goose that laid the golden egg," commented Tere in January 1965, as we walked around the building together before the beginning of the new term. "Every year there are more students and we add another classroom, and now we have a courtyard!"

It was true. A tall poinsettia bush that had been just outside the bungalow now spread its red leaves over the grassy patch at the center of the courtyard, and all around, a covered veranda led to doors opening onto three classrooms and three typing rooms. Green vines of golden shower, with their drooping orange flowers gleaming in the sunlight, climbed the thin stone pillars, ran along the red corrugated iron roof, and spilled over onto the cream-colored walls.

"Kianda is lovely, isn't it?" Tere continued. "No matter what happens, we will always keep this place." She was dreading the "monster" we were about to build.

With girls applying to Kianda from all over eastern Africa and beyond on account of the sponsorship program, that one floor of one of the women's halls at the Royal Technical College became inadequate, especially since more female students were also applying to that institution. It became imperative for Kianda to have its own residence, so plans were made for a building that would accommodate a hundred students and staff. We were already committed to the project and the blueprints had been made, but we had to raise funds. One place we applied to was the Ford Foundation, where Mr. Frank Sutton gave us invaluable help. He believed in our project and showed us how to present it in the language of donors.

We realized that most of the funding would have to come from abroad. We applied to several organizations in Germany which helped fund projects for women's development in Third World countries. Tere was also following up some contacts in Spain. However, the money was slow in coming.

"One of these days we'll go to prison for not meeting our debts," she said, only half joking.

"Why doesn't Tere go to Europe and follow up our requests?" suggested Cuca. "It makes a much greater impact when you talk to people in person."

Tere agreed. "I would really like to go," she said. "The worst is just to sit waiting for something to happen."

Tere and Cuca visited our manager at the Ottoman Bank to discuss the possibility of a loan. He was a hard-headed Scotsman, and they had to plead our case. Finally he told Tere, "If you can raise funds overseas, the bank will match the amount fifty-fifty in the form of a loan."

That settled it. Tere prepared to travel to Europe. She was understandably nervous the day she set out on the fundraising trip, and we promised to back her up with our prayers.

On her way to Germany she stopped in Rome, and there she repeated her comment about going to prison for debt. Someone must have told the Father about it, because that evening, when he came to give her his blessing, he brought a heap of little Murano glass ducks and put them in her hands, saying that these were the vocations that would come from the future residence . . . and that there would be no prison.

The trip was successful. A German foundation, built up with funds contributed by the German people, agreed to finance the building, and Tere came back with an armload of studies that had to be done. She was also given donations by people in Spain, starting with her own family.

"After one talk I gave about Kianda," she told us, "a

couple came and handed me an envelope. 'We discussed it together,' the husband said, 'and we all agreed to go without our summer vacation this year so that the money can go to Kianda instead.'"

Our Kenyan friends also helped with their contributions and prayers. One evening Pamela Mboya called to say, "I thought you would like to know that I was just saying night prayers with the children, and Maureen reminded me, 'Mommy, we haven't prayed for Aunty Olga's school!'"

Passy Roche, the sister of another Luo friend of mine, had a very serious heart condition which kept her housebound. To help build Kianda Residence she asked people to bring her their empty bottles and old newspapers, which she then sold. Every month, with a radiant smile, she pressed into my hand some shillings "for Kianda."

Our students also helped. Elizabeth Wanjera had returned to Kianda for a refresher course, and one morning she came to my office with an envelope, saying, "I'm bringing you half of this month's salary for Kianda."

"But how will you manage, Elizabeth?" I asked. "Your family needs the money. You can help us with your prayers."

"I'm already doing that," she answered. "I want to help financially. If it wasn't for Kianda and everything I learned here, I wouldn't have any salary at all."

I wrote to our alumnae telling them about the residence and asking for their collaboration. One of them, Mary Maina, wrote back, "I was so happy that you asked me to help with your future plans, because I always knew in my heart that I owe Kianda everything I am as a secretary and as a woman. What could I do more than just say 'thanks'? My parents also asked me many times, 'How can we show our appreciation to Kianda for all they did for you?' and I didn't know what to answer. When your letter came asking for help, my heart jumped for joy. It is a chance to give the little I have. I'm enclosing half my salary for this month, and next month I'll send you another half. My mother is sending you vegetables from the garden."

On Saturday, February 26, 1966, the contractor came on-site, his bulldozers went to work, and the groundbreaking began. We watched as the foundations were laid, the pillars were set, and the building gradually came up. While the flat architectural drawings became a three-dimensional reality, we gave our classes to the accompaniment of tractors and bulldozers.

Not long after construction began, the foreman, a turbaned Indian Singh, came to ask for information about the school. "I have seen how happy the students are here," he said, "and I want to send my daughter next term."

When the four-story residence was practically finished, we thought about having an official opening, and I discussed this with Mrs. Gecaga.

"For such an occasion," she said, "you could invite Her Excellency Mama Ngina Kenyatta to perform the opening ceremony. I'm sure she would be willing to come."

With the help of Mrs. Gecaga and Mrs. Rubia everything was set in motion, and confirmation came that the First Lady would unveil a commemorative stone at Kianda on October 28, 1966. The event was handled from the state capitol and planned down to the last detail. It was to be Mama Ngina's first public engagement since Jomo Kenyatta's inauguration as President of the Republic of Kenya in 1964.

We sent out invitations to dignitaries and friends and had the stone prepared, as well as a red curtain and cord for Mama Ngina to draw when the time came. A dais with a flowered canopy was set up in front of the building.

On the morning of October 28 Kianda was a hive of activity with officials from the state capitol coming and going, our gardeners (including Nyawira, who had come with us from Invergara) setting up rows of chairs in front of the dais, Cuca getting her camera ready, and some Kibondeni staff and students preparing the tea. A TV van drove up and stationed itself strategically at a discreet distance from the dais.

By 3:00 the place was filled with people of all ages, races, and social classes chatting animatedly as they admired the building and waited for the ceremony to begin. I was happy to see Mrs. Rosemary White in the first row, with her friend Lady Madge Harragin, and I stopped to talk with them. I had met Lady Harragin on a number of occasions, and she admired the work we were doing. Now she said to me, very emotionally, "It is a wonderful thing to meet people who dream dreams and then make those dreams a reality!"

At 3:00 Tere and I stood at the entrance to Kianda College, ready to move forward when the First Lady arrived. As time passed I grew more and more nervous. The main speech was to be given by the Assistant Minister of Education, Mr. John Konchellah, and he had not turned up yet. I had prepared our thank-you speech, which I held in moist hands, but if he didn't come I would have to give both speeches, and I trembled at the thought.

Suddenly presidential escort motorcycles turned in through the gate and roared up the drive, headlights on, followed at a more leisurely pace by the flag-fluttering limousine bearing Mama Ngina. We went forward to meet her, and just as I held out my hand to greet the First Lady, I found Mr. Konchellah standing beside me, beaming as if nothing had happened. I heaved a sigh of relief. Mama Ngina was very elegant and had a charming smile and easy manner. We walked down the path towards the dais, and in front of the residence I introduced the Kianda College staff. Mama Ngina shook hands with them, one by one, and had a warm smile for each.

In his speech the Assistant Minister of Education said, "It is a great honor for me to be here this afternoon together with the friends of Kianda, adding one more step to the rapid progress of this college, which in just a few years has set the standard for how to teach in this kind of institution. . . . The Government and especially my Ministry wants not only to thank the managers, but also to offer them our support and our esteem."

Then I gave our talk. "Kianda," I said, "is a family home in which each person is encouraged to answer responsibly for her rights and duties. The staff aim not only at producing good and competent secretaries, but at educating their students so as to enable them to fulfill their roles in society, both in the office and in the family."

The moment had come for Mama Ngina to unveil the commemorative stone. Together we walked over to the main door of the new residence while everyone waited expectantly. We stood beside the curtain, Mama Ngina pulled the cord . . . and nothing happened. She tried several times, while I blushed with embarrassment, and then, with a hearty laugh, she caught up the curtain in her hand and pulled it aside, revealing the stone, amidst loud applause and cheering from the guests.

Tere and I then gave the First Lady a tour around the four-story residence, and at the end we stepped out onto the flat roof overlooking Nairobi and the Ngong Hills. "A beautiful building!" she exclaimed several times. In the main hall I introduced to her the architect, who in turn presented the contractor and others involved in the construction of the residence. Then we went to Kianda College for tea. After a short stay, Mama Ngina returned to her limousine, and the presidential escort departed with a flourish. That night the event received ten minutes of news coverage on TV, and on the following day it was amply reported in the newspapers.

Now that the building was ready, the work of furnishing and decorating began. Tere had a file where she kept addresses of auctioneers, furniture stores, and contacts, and lists of available items and their prices, and she constantly updated it. "In case I die, you have all the information there," she told Cuca.

Tere and Cuca worked out a budget for furnishing the residence and spent hours crouched on the floor beside the outspread architectural drawings, moving cut-to-size pieces of variously colored manila paper representing beds, tables, chairs, nightstands, and so on, to see what could fit in each room.

Sol Goyoaga and Pilu Herrán were in charge of the interior decorating. They supervised the making of curtains and matching bedspreads and prepared pictures for framing. The bedrooms for three and for five were large and airy, with a closet for each occupant.

The common room extended the whole length of the main corridor and had windows all along that side. Its red tiled floor, designed to ward off stiletto heel marks, was relieved by patterned Italian tiles. The wall opposite the corridor had windows overlooking a garden courtyard. In the center of that wall was the pièce de résistance: a large, open stone fireplace which dominated the whole room.

The first sixty residents arrived in January 1967. They were of all races and of different tribes of Kenya and other African countries. In the next thirty years seven thousand students would pass through Kianda, from forty-eight countries including seventeen in Africa.

We had girls from different races share rooms so that they could more easily interrelate. One English girl showed reluctance to share a room with an African. "I don't like Africans," she said bluntly. A couple of weeks later I asked her how she was doing and if she felt the same, and she replied, "I still feel the same, only the African girl in my room is different. I like her."

Another European resident confided that she felt ashamed of herself. "We were discussing pocket money last night," she said, "and I complained that Dad doesn't give me enough. I asked Wanjiru about her pocket money, and she said that she gets it from her sponsors and then sends it all home for the education of her little brothers and sisters."

There were several Tanzanians in Kianda Residence, among them "the two Anastasias." They not only shared the same name but came from the same little island in Lake Victoria, and both were very shy and retiring. Somehow we couldn't get through to them, and they weren't doing well. One day there was a get-together after dinner and everyone was asked to do something. The two Anastasias disappeared for a while and then returned wearing long Tanzanian dresses and dancing and singing in Swahili with such vigor, rhythm, and enthusiasm that the whole room joined in. From that moment on they were different people; they had come alive, and started doing well in class and relating with the other students.

Musical get-togethers became a feature of Kianda Residence. Pilu got out her guitar and sang Mexican songs; past students of the school in Limuru, headed by Mary Kibera, danced Irish reels, wearing plaid skirts, white blouses, and diagonal, over-the-shoulder colored bands; two Greek residents danced to the haunting theme song of *Zorba the Greek*; the Indian girls danced solos, wearing magnificent silk outfits in dazzling colors, their arms and bare feet covered with bangles and little bells; and the two Anastasias, wearing colorful kangas, led African dances.

In 1968 we had to make our first payment on the Ottoman Bank loan, and we didn't have the money, so Tere set everyone praying to our holy intercessor Saint Nicholas while we looked for ways to raise funds.

The residents came up with a suggestion: "We were thinking that we could give a concert to raise money, polishing up the songs and dances from the get-togethers."

"That's a good idea," I said, touched at their thoughtfulness. "But where will you have it? The living room is too small."

"We were thinking of asking for the Hospital Hill school hall."

"All right, you go ahead and set it up."

They did, and the concert was a great success from all points of view. The proceeds helped us solve the financial problem and the audience was most entertained. A TV producer from the Kenya Broadcasting Company was there, and she invited the girls to perform for television.

Christmas was still reflected little in the media, so we thought of preparing a Christmas program for television. I made an appointment to see Eulalia Onyango, one of the producers, and she was very encouraging. "Work out a script, music, and visuals," she said, "and then contact me again."

The atmosphere at the KBC studios fascinated me, and the idea that we could prepare a program at Kianda that would actually be televised fired me with enthusiasm. I had an equally enthusiastic collaborator in Ernie Vanderlin, a mother of six, from Madison, Wisconsin, who was then teaching English on a volunteer basis at Kianda College. The two of us put together an ambitious project, a two-installment program called "The Joys of Christmas."

Eulalia Onyango approved the script and booked the dates for recording and viewing, and we set to work in earnest. The students threw themselves into the venture wholeheartedly, mustering all their talents. Linda Aves led the choir, which prepared polyphonic Christmas carols in different languages. Serah Mwangi was the host. Marilyn d'Souza demonstrated the setting up of a Nativity set, assisted by Mary Kibera's little sister Rose and Ernie's youngest daughter, Pammie. Ernie also taught one of the students how to make and present the making of a "sweet wreath" by pulling a coat hanger into circular shape, stringing it with *peremende* (wrapped candies) until it was thick with them, and then hanging a pair of scissors over the hook so that anyone could cut one off at Christmastime. The girls demonstrated Christmas baking, how to decorate a tree, how to make a Christmas card . . . Nothing was omitted.

It was exciting to watch the recording in the TV studios. We brought from home everything for our stage sets, including crèche, tree, and decorations, and once all these were placed at different angles on the studio floor, everyone took up her place, the choir standing on graded benches. Then the lighting and the microphones were adjusted while Eulalia gave last-minute instructions before vanishing into the control room upstairs. The huge cameras moved silently around the brightly lit studio, taking the shots Eulalia called for. From my place in the wings I could hear her voice coming through the cameramen's earphones as she rapidly snapped out cues. Ernie and I sat watching breathlessly until it was all over.

The programs were televised, and in addition to bringing the Christmas message into many homes, they also brought more inquiries about Kianda College. An unexpected bonus came in the form of a modest check from KBC for our work.

A few days before Christmas, I was in a store and I ran into two friends who were there to buy blunt scissors. "For the sweet wreath!" they exclaimed. "Our children and their friends are really going to enjoy this."

Only one store in town sold Nativity sets, and they had very few in stock. "Next time please tell me well in advance when you intend to advertise the Nativity set," the owner said. "Shipments from Europe take six months to arrive, and these days we're getting nothing but requests for those sets."

The Kianda Christmas Program became an annual event—one of the many dreams to come true at Kianda over the years.

* 16 *

Tom Mboya

Tom Mboya continued to be a good friend to Kianda College. As Minister of Economic Planning and Development he signed many letters of recommendation for our project requests. When the work permit situation became difficult and I decided to apply for Kenyan citizenship, he vouched for me.

In 1968 Tom Mboya, accompanied by his wife, paid an official visit to Kianda Residence and presented the students with a record player. In his speech he said, "The most important task is that of helping to develop healthy, intelligent, and creative young people, people who will play an important part in the development of our nation, and the development of our nation includes its moral and spiritual development.

"There must be certain values in man, certain principles, certain ideals, and certain standards of behavior. We in the Government are very happy with the products of Kianda College in every department in which they have been employed. I have not heard any word of criticism. Kianda College has taken her place among the most distinguished secretarial colleges."

Around that time I was introduced to Joan Argwings Kodhek, the wife of a Catholic member of the Kenyan government. As she herself was not a Catholic, Joan wanted to learn about her husband's religion in order to look after the religious upbringing of her children.

She had come for several doctrinal classes when suddenly one morning I read in the newspaper that her husband had died under very strange circumstances. Although I had never met him, it was a shock, and I went to her home to express my condolences.

That death was the first of several that were to rock the nation.

Joan's home was in the residential area of Lavington. As I drew near, I heard screaming and yelling from the streets as wailing women, flinging themselves about, made their way to the house. I found it frightening and eerie. I went in to condole with Joan, who lay on her bed surrounded by attentive women in mourning. I didn't stay long, as I didn't know what to do. A week later I attended the funeral Mass at Holy Family Cathedral. It was so packed that I had to stand squashed against a pillar, unable to see anything.

The whole thing distressed me, and I asked Pamela Mboya about it the next time we met. "There are many traditions and practices connected with Luo funerals," she told me. "Women wail to show their grief, and the widow and her children have their heads shaved. Since the wife belongs to her husband's clan and a woman must not remain single and unprotected, she has to pass, with her children and the property, to the eldest surviving brother."

"You mean she becomes his wife?" I asked.

"Yes," Pamela replied.

"What if he's already married?"

"Then she becomes a second or third wife. And she is expected to bear another child in honor of her dead husband. Women don't have any say in the matter; they have no rights. The woman must do what the clan expects of her."

It sounded very sad to me. "She has no say over herself or the property or her children?"

"No," said Pamela. "She doesn't qualify to own anything. She came into the clan upon marriage and usually cannot leave it." Then she added, shaking her head, "The most unhappy woman in the world is the Luo widow."

Little did we know that within a few months she herself would be widowed in such a tragic way.

In June 1969 Maureen, now nearly seven, was to make her First Holy Communion. I asked Mother to send me a gold cross and chain for her. Pamela wouldn't be able to attend the ceremony, as she had an engagement in Europe, but she prepared everything (white dress, gloves, veil) and asked me to come and get the child ready. When the Sunday arrived, I went to the Mboyas' house to dress Maureen, and I hung the little gold cross around her neck. Then she got into the car with Tom, Peter, and Susan, and I followed them to Holy Family Cathedral for Mass. That was the last time I saw Tom.

On Saturday, July 5, I was at work in Kianda Residence when, just after twelve, a Luo friend, Margaret Arara, telephoned. Obviously very shaken, she could only keep saying, "Our friend has been shot! Our friend has been shot!" At first I couldn't understand what she meant, and then it dawned on me that she was talking about Tom Mboya. "Is it very bad?" I asked, shocked. Margaret answered, "Very." "I'm coming right away," I said, and hurried to her home. People were rapidly congregating in the Araras' ground-floor apartment in Nairobi South "B," and there I learned the whole story.

Tom had been assassinated on his way out of a pharmacy on Government Road. He had been rushed to the hospital, but nothing could be done; the bullet had pierced the aorta, and he died within an hour. He was thirty-nine. I prayed for him and for the family, while trying to assimilate the fact that evil forces had snatched Tom from us. One of the visitors told me that the children had been taken to the home of a relative, so I went there and tried to comfort them.

That evening Pamela sent a car and driver to Kianda for me. When I arrived at the house, I found her lying on the bed, dazed and grief-stricken, while visitors came in and out to condole with her. We talked a little, she repeated to me what had happened, and she asked me to look after the children. I told her I had already been to see them and would go again. After giving her what comfort I could, I went to pray in front of Tom's body, which was laid out in the living room. Crowds of people were gathered there, mourning and weeping. I said a Rosary in front of the open coffin. The body looked somehow shrunken, while the face was just a shell. From time to time a man came up and stroked it—the deepest form of male mourning.

I was shaken by the event, very personally and deeply affected. From the beginning Tom had supported Kianda and everything we stood for, and his influence had often been decisive. He had always been there for us—and now there was only a vacuum. That night I stayed up late writing a long letter to the Father, telling him everything that had happened. I knew he would suffer with us and pray for Tom and his family.

The next day I returned to Pamela's house to find everything in an upheaval. People had arrived from up-country, there was wailing and weeping in the streets, and, to my horror, I saw people carrying away all kinds of family possessions from the home—a photograph of Tom, knickknacks, chairs . . . It seemed to me like a desecration.

The day of the funeral arrived. I went with the Secretary of Wildlife and Tourism, Alois Achieng, and his wife, Mary. The streets were thronged, and the crowd thickened as we approached the cathedral. It was at the same time a grief-stricken and a menacing crowd, a potent sign of the discontent always simmering just below the surface of a country that had yet to find true nationhood above tribal affiliations. The fragile unity between juxtaposed tribal communities had yet to solidify in our young nation. People had to learn to be Kenyan. Tom was truly Kenyan.

We made our way into the cathedral, which was soon packed. When everyone was inside, the huge copper doors were locked—something that almost never happens.

Sitting a few pews ahead of me were President Kenyatta and Mama Ngina, and on the other side of the aisle, the Mboya family. The coffin lay on the marble floor of the sanctuary, covered with wreaths of flowers. Everything in the cathedral was very dignified; but outside there was chaos.

People were shouting angrily. There was rioting, with gunshots that were followed by tear gas which made its way into the cathedral. The congregation coughed into handkerchiefs. Those watching the service on TV thought that everyone was crying. I was frightened and asked Alois tremulously, "Will we be all right?" "I don't know," he whispered back. That didn't make me feel any better.

Archbishop John Joseph McCarthy was wonderful. He celebrated the Mass with great solemnity and gave the homily without paying the slightest attention to the commotion outside. When we finally emerged from the cathedral there was no one around, but a pall hung over the city—a mixture of tear gas, gunpowder, and that something which hangs in the air after a tragedy. Here and there I caught sight of an abandoned shoe, bits and pieces of torn cloth . . . I was very glad to get home that evening.

The assassin was later caught and brought to justice, but that could never bring back this man of such intelligence and stature. It was a wound in the side of the nation that would take a long time to heal. For trust had been broken, and trust is a fragile thing.

17

Growth of Our Family

By 1971 Kianda Residence had become central to all our activities. As members of Kenya's Regional Advisory (the governing body of Opus Dei women), Tere, Charo Basterra, and I lived and worked in three independent rooms on the first floor. We had on that floor a carving of Our Lady, Queen of Kenya, which the Father had blessed for us, and at her feet were the little ducks he had given to Tere. The persons that had come to the Work already outnumbered the ducks.

Ursula Okondo, a Luhya from western Kenya, was brought up in a devout Catholic family. Her father was the first catechist in his area and had been honored with a medal from the Pope. Gaitano and his wife educated a family of nine children. Ursula first heard about Kianda College when Tere and Cuca visited the Mukumu Girls' Secondary School, where she was a student, and she decided to apply. Her eldest brother, Peter, brought her for the interview, and Ursula entered Kianda the following term.

Ursula made great friends with Tere and asked her many questions about the Work. "When I was young," she said, "I would tell my mother that I wanted to stay with her and my father always, because I wanted to work for God but not as a Sister—I didn't quite know in what way. She told me she would be happy to have any of her daughters stay at home if they didn't want to get married, but then she asked me, 'What would you do, staying here with me all your life?' I answered, 'Maybe I could bring up orphan children to be good Catholics.' I hadn't heard about Opus Dei then."

Ursula wrote to tell her parents that she was thinking of joining the Work, and her father came to Nairobi to find out about it. She and Tere explained Opus Dei to him, and he listened cautiously, not totally satisfied. It was only on his way out, when he was shown a picture of the Pope with the Father, that he exclaimed, "The Holy Father approves of it? Then I give you my blessing!" On December 8, 1965, Ursula asked to be admitted to Opus Dei.

Dorina Telaide was of Italian ancestry but was born in Ethiopia and came to Kenya with her family at the age of three. She finished school at the end of 1964 and was debating with herself what career to go into when one of her Italian friends, Wanda La Magna, a student at Kianda, talked to her about the college.

"There must be something special about that place," Dorina thought to herself, "because Wanda doesn't stop talking about it." Wanda brought her an application and urged her to fill it out. "Don't think twice about it," she said. "The courses there will always come in handy, even if afterwards you go into teaching, as you're planning." So Dorina applied. The day before the term began, Wanda invited Dorina to spend the day with her at Kianda. "But what will we do there? Classes haven't started yet," said Dorina. Wanda laughed. "I'm telling you," she said, "it's not an ordinary college. You feel at home and they always have something for you to do. Don't worry, you won't be bored!"

Wanda was right, Dorina wasn't bored. In no time the girls were busy hanging curtains in a classroom that had just been added to make room for more students. There was a lot of work because the contractor had delayed in handing over the room, and the two remained till evening helping to finish off the last details. "Ink, chalk, eraser . . . Count the chairs and tables. This room is for thirty students . . . ," called out Tere, who was directing the operation. Dorina was surprised to see how, despite the speed with which everything had to be done, attention was paid to details like setting a picture straight, placing a decoration in the right spot, putting flowers in vases . . .

The months went by, and on October 2, the anniversary of the founding of Opus Dei, Dorina attended the principal's talk about the Work. "I feel sure that this is for me," she afterwards confided to her friend Pilu.

"Have you ever thought about a vocation before?" asked Pilu, surprised.

"No," Dorina replied. "But I didn't know about Opus Dei before."

"There is a retreat next month, why don't you go?" suggested Pilu. "We can talk more about it afterwards." Dorina did go, and on December 6, 1965, she wrote her letter to the Father asking admission to the Work.

Dorina didn't like the idea of leaving Kianda, so I asked her if she would be interested in studying for certification as a teacher of typing and shorthand after gaining some months' experience in an office. She was delighted at the prospect. "I can come back to Kianda," she said, "and also be what I always wanted—a teacher!"

Other alumnae followed Dorina's example and studied for the business teachers' diplomas, and of those who joined the Kianda staff, some became members of the Work. Ten years after her arrival in Kenya, Constance Gillan was able to comment, with a twinkle in her Irish eyes, "I taught these girls and now I have the pleasure of seeing that they are better teachers than I am."

At a meeting of the Nairobi Classical Society, Mila met Joan Gilmartin. A veterinarian, Joan had come to Kenya from Queensland, Australia, to do some research. Mila invited her to visit Kianda, and she was impressed with the work being done there. She began to take part in the days of recollection and other activities and eventually asked admission to Opus Dei.

Joan became the director of Kianda Residence, and the girls had a great affection for her. She was usually to be found standing outside the door of her office, knitting in hand, with a ready ear for everyone.

Ursula went to the University of Navarre, in Pamplona, Spain, for further studies. There she met the Father for the first time. As Ursula was the only African in the university residence and was so far from home, Merche Goyarrola wrote to her parents, who lived in nearby Bilbao, asking them to look after her. They went to visit her in Pamplona, invited her to their home, and treated her like a daughter. Merche received a letter from her mother saying, "Having Ursula here is almost like having you." When Ursula finally returned home, Merche's mother complained, "Kenya is robbing us of all our daughters!"

While Ursula was in Spain, her brother Peter, who was now head of the family since Gaitano had passed away, called an important family meeting at which every member had to be present. He contacted Tere so that she could attend on behalf of Ursula—recognizing that we were really a family.

We visited and got to know the families of new members of the Work and were happy to find that so many parents understood that in giving a daughter to God in Opus Dei they had gained another family.

The Father's concern reached to every aspect of this family. After *uhuru* the concept of "houseboy" disappeared and domestic and catering jobs became open to women as well as men. However, the living conditions were not suited to this new situation, since the "houseboys' quarters" had one bedroom per person, but communal toilet and cooking facilities. The Father asked us to find a way to provide suitable accommodations in Nairobi for the Kibondeni alumnae who were working there.

Margaret Arara's husband was on the Nairobi City Council, and I thought he might be able to suggest something. The couple were amazed when I told them what we were looking for and why.

"Do you mean the Father knows about the Kibondeni girls and is even concerned about their accommodations?" Margaret couldn't get over it. "Just leave it to us," she said. "My husband and I will look for a suitable place."

The Araras combed the area where they lived, and eventually they discovered a disused private nursing home, not far from their own home. That was the beginning of Watani Hostel, a residence for working girls.

In January 1971 we received an invitation to participate in the Incontro Romano, an international youth conference to be held in Rome at Easter. The program included an audience with the Pope and a get-together with the Father. The Incontro had been taking place for several years, but we had never considered participating, as the airfare made it too expensive.

One morning, as I stood waiting for the light at Mama Ngina Street to change, I was thinking about this and was wishing that we could give the Father the joy of meeting a group of his Kenya daughters. Joan was the first Australian, and if she could go, the Father would for the first time be surrounded by daughters of his from five continents.

Suddenly my attention was caught by a large neon advertisement on the top of a nearby building: "FLY EAST AFRICAN AIRWAYS." The thought came to my mind that we could propose to the airline that they fly a group to Rome in exchange for advertising. We could put together a TV program for KBC (where we were already known from our Christmas programs) in which the participants would relate their Rome experiences and thank East African Airways for making the journey possible. I could hardly wait to get home and suggest the idea to the others.

"It's a great idea," Tere said thoughtfully, "but who do we know at East African Airways? You can't just go there without the backing of someone."

"What about Pamela Mboya? She knows lots of people," I said. I asked her about it, and she contacted one of her sisters, who gave me the name of a Luo manager at EAA. After several visits and discussions he offered us fifteen tickets: five at full fare, five at half fare, and five for free.

We juggled things around so that all fifteen participants—members of the Work and friends—paid something and benefited from the sponsorship. Excitement was at fever pitch at Kianda as the girls got ready to travel, many for the first time: Worke and Azeb Fesseha, sisters from Ethiopia; Marilyn and Sylvia d'Souza, of Indian origin; Joan Gilmartin, from Australia; Serah Mwangi, Berni Okondo, Teresia Wairimu Njuguna, Christine Gichure, and Rosemary Mboya, Kenyans; Charo Basterra, from Spain . . . The Africans and Indians prepared national dresses and saris to wear on the great occasions, and we made a harambee to collect warm clothes for all of them, borrowing from friends. They left by two different flights, on April 2 and 4.

The group spent a week in Rome, where they stayed in student hostels with girls from many other parts of the world. Besides participating in the activities of the Incontro conference, they attended the Holy Week services at St. Peter's, visited historic sites in Rome, and had an audience with the Pope. The students were also received in groups by the Father, who admired the colorful national dresses of the girls in the Kenyan group.

In that get-together Serah Mwangi thanked the Father for having sent the Work to Kenya, and he replied, "It is our Lord who sent Opus Dei to Africa. I am a poor instrument of God, and you must pray that I may be a good and faithful instrument. Now Opus Dei has to spread all over Africa, but with Africans. You must spread the love of God generously all over your continent. Be pious, follow the way by which God leads you, whatever it may be, matrimony if he calls you to that state. And don't say no to grace if you feel the restless impulse to give yourselves completely, because then our Lord is showing you that he wants more."

"Father, we have come here from five continents," said Marilyn. "How is it that the Work has spread so far and so quickly?"

"It is because God made it essentially universal and willed that we be threshed at the beginning like wheat is threshed, with blows that extract the grain from the ear. That is what happened to the Work, and so the wind of God's grace carried the seed to the five continents."

"When will you come to Kenya, Father?" Marilyn asked, with a persuasive smile.

"Whenever our Lord wants. But I can assure you, I am longing to go."

"And when will the Work go to Ethiopia?" added Azeb.

"We need more Ethiopian vocations. Look at the miracle our Lord has worked in Kenya. Americans and Europeans went there . . . and he has given us African vocations. But we can't try to force God to work miracles. That is why many vocations are needed from Kenya, Nigeria, Ethiopia—all of Africa!—to sow peace and joy on your continent."

As the Father rose to leave the room, Rosemary Mboya stepped forward and put in his hands a soapstone duck she had brought for him from Kenya. He was very touched and said, "My daughter, I couldn't love you more than I do! Why do you give me this?"

The group returned from Rome radiant. Moreover, Charo brought a totally unexpected message from the Father.

18

Expanding to West Africa

"The Father wants you to stop in Rome on your way to the States," Charo told me, smiling broadly. "And he also wants you to visit Nigeria on your way back!"

"What?" I sat down abruptly on the bed, beside my open suitcase, and stared at Charo. The excitement of the return of the first group from Rome had just subsided and I was preparing for traveling that night to England and, after some days there, to the United States, to visit my parents.

Tere stood behind Charo, wide-eyed. "You'll have to get a visa for Nigeria," she said. "Isn't it lucky that we have a Nigerian student at Kianda? I'm sure Rhona will introduce you to some people who can help."

This wasn't the first I had heard about Nigeria. Soon after Audrey Leitch went there in 1963 I received a letter from her describing their house in Lagos and her impressions of the country. "It is hot and humid, more tropical than Kenya," she wrote. "We don't have flowers in the garden, but there are huge plants with colorful leaves. . . . You must come here. I think a secretarial college like Kianda would be very welcome in Lagos."

Then we received from Carlette Roeske, who had been such an asset to Kianda, a letter saying that Pim had been assigned to Lagos and so they were moving there. I sent her Father Gabiola's address and asked her to contact him. She did, but she also sent us insistent letters saying, "Why don't you come to Lagos yourself? You can stay with us. We need a Kianda in Nigeria."

Now the Father himself wanted us to go to Nigeria.

"I must write to Carlette," I said. "She'll be delighted." Then I added, "Imagine, Tere, I'm going to Rome!"

"You lucky thing!" she exclaimed.

Rhona Nabeta introduced me to Nigeria's High Commissioner, Mr. Ignatius Olisemeka, and his wife, Gloria. They were very encouraging and helpful. "A secretarial college like Kianda can make a good contribution to women's education in Nigeria," Gloria told me, "but you must consider carefully what kind of diplomas you are going to offer. Our people are accustomed to studying abroad and want British certifications. As far as I know, the City & Guilds diplomas are the most recognized in Nigeria." She gave me letters of introduction to the President's wife, Mrs. Victoria Gowon, and to the principal of the government secretarial college.

On May 15, 1971, I set out for Rome, the first lap of my journey. "Give our love to the Father and tell him we are praying for Nigeria," Tere said as she and Charo waved me off at Jomo Kenyatta Airport.

I couldn't help recalling the Strathmore "Home again!" song as I emerged from the taxi at Villa Sacchetti and pressed the doorbell. Although there were many new faces, the atmosphere there was just the same as before. Everyone was talking about the recent Incontro and the novelty of Kenyans participating for the first time, and how happy the Father was. "When will I see him?" I asked. "Probably tomorrow," they told me.

The following morning I was praying in the oratory when someone came looking for me. "The Father wants to see you in the meeting room in five minutes!" she said. I hurried to that room and waited near the big mahogany table with the rose-colored velvet chairs around it, and soon I heard the unmistakable voice of the Father. He came in accompanied by Don Alvaro, Mercedes Morado, and Marlies Kücking.

"Pax, Olga, my daughter! How happy I am to see you," he said, and then invited us all to sit down around the table.

The Father said how happy he was with the group that

had come from Kenya and mentioned that the two Ethiopians had brought a processional cross from their country. He told me how well our Kenyans in Rome were doing. "They are splendid!" he said.

Then he asked with great interest about my parents, how old they were now and where they were living. I was glad to be able to talk to him about them. I told him that my father was Jewish and had suffered a lot on account of this. The Father immediately exclaimed, "Jesus and Mary were—are—Jews!" He told me to give my father a big hug for him and to tell my parents that he loved them very much and asked that they pray for him and for Africa. Then he brought out a rosary and a bronze medallion of the Roman College, blessed them, and gave me the rosary for my father to keep as a present from him, even though he wouldn't use it, and the medallion for my mother, saying that since it was blessed, she would gain an indulgence every time she looked at it raising her heart to God. Before giving me his blessing, the Father told me to pray very much for the work in Kenya and Nigeria.

At Wickenden Manor I found that Anna Barret and Carmen Torrente were two of the people who would be taking with me the summer course deepening our Christian formation and our understanding of the spirit of the Work. Both of them were living and working in England. Carmen told me about a Ugandan friend of hers named Catherine Omaswa. "She and her husband are doctors," she said, "and are very fine people. They have just returned to Africa and are living in Nairobi. Do you think you could look them up?" I promised to do so.

At Wickenden I received several letters from ladies in Ibadan. Fola Olumide sent a full report about the educational system in Nigeria and added, "I hope to be able to persuade you to come to Ibadan to meet my family and friends. I have been interested in Opus Dei for a long time, especially ever since I found out that married women can be admitted. We would all like you to come visit us. The priests of the Work are doing a very good job. I hope to meet you soon so you can tell me how you joined Opus Dei."

I called the City & Guilds office from Wickenden to see if I could get an appointment to discuss possible courses for a college in Lagos. When I gave my name, the secretary exclaimed, "Miss Marlin? From Kenya? I was your student at Kianda!" And she facilitated everything for me.

In London I was able to get together with my three sisters, who were all now married and living there. Brigid and I had agreed to meet in a bookshop, and as I stood diffidently studying the shelves, she came through the door in arty attire and to my great discomfiture rushed at me with open arms, crying "Olgie!" Then we both laughed. We spent the day together and fell easily into our old companionable relationship. "Isn't it funny," Brigid said, "no matter how many years go by, every time we get together we take up just where we left off."

At teatime we made our way to Liz's hospital. "We mustn't disturb her during office hours," Brigid had said. "She's a very important person, you know." On our way up to her office I prepared myself to meet again this little sister who was now a married woman and a prestigious medical doctor. We entered the room and there she was, behind the desk in her white coat. After the first excited greetings we looked shyly at one another. She didn't seem to me to have changed at all from the twelve-year-old I had last seen—the girl with the serene, penetrating brown eyes, firm chin, and general air of self-possession. Liz picked up the phone and said, "Please send up tea for three." Then, bubbling over in a heartwarming way, she added, "My sister is here from Africa!"

Sheila took me to her home in Berkhamsted for dinner. "I'm afraid the house is upside down at present," she said apologetically, "but my girls are into everything, and with my Montessori school right next door, I simply can't keep the house tidy." With a little laugh and a sigh, she brushed the hair from her forehead. Sheila was a born manager. She had always taken on more than one would think she could handle and had made it work.

I traveled by PanAm to D.C. and found my parents waiting eagerly for me at the airport. Daddy enfolded me in his arms, while Mother beamed and kissed me on both cheeks. "Isn't this lovely!" she exclaimed.

It was very hot and humid, and a yellow haze hung in the air. "We're in the middle of a heat wave," Daddy said as he drove through the traffic. I tried to recognize the landmarks he pointed out to me, but everything felt strange. With the time lag my body told me it was the wee hours of the morning, while my watch showed early evening. I had a kind of "white nights" sensation.

As soon as we arrived home, Mother announced, "I have a surprise for you!" She disappeared into the kitchen and then returned with a big bowl of cherries. "I bet you never have these in Africa!" she said triumphantly. Indeed we didn't. "I also have surprises for you," I said. Then I told them about my meeting with the Father and gave them the gifts and the messages. Mother was particularly pleased with the medallion and immediately placed it on her nightstand. The photos I brought of their four daughters together in England also made them very happy.

Daddy drove Mother and me to New York City, where we visited the rest of the family: John, with his fiancée, Alice; and Randal, who had come from Canada with his wife, Elaine, and their baby daughter, Christine. I realized with a pang that my brothers now had lives and families of their own, apart from me. Just as I, too, had my own life . . .

When I departed on the Pan Am flight for Lagos, I expected the journey eastward to be less tiring, because of the short night, but it didn't happen that way. Our first stop was supposed to be Rabat, Morocco, but because of a coup there, we were rerouted to Lisbon for a six-hour delay.

When the plane finally landed in Lagos, we emerged to a hot, sultry evening and made our way to the long hangar which was Lagos Airport. After going through all the formalities, I went out to find a beaming Carlette and Pim waiting for me. "Welcome to Nigeria!" they said. "How was your trip?"

We piled into their blue Volkswagen, and while Pim drove through the town I looked out the window, fascinated. It was very different from Nairobi. The streets were thronged with noisy, gesticulating people, and billboards were everywhere. "They all have African faces," I commented, surprised. "Oh yes, Nigeria is completely African," replied Carlette.

Lagos was linked to the mainland and to the islands of Victoria and Ikoyi by bridges, and the traffic was so heavy that for some time we were stopped on one of them. "It can take a couple of hours for these bottlenecks to clear," said Pim. "I go to work very early in the morning so I can leave early and avoid the rush-hour traffic. On a Sunday it takes ten minutes to cross Lagos, but the same trip may take three or four hours on weekdays."

No one seemed impatient. The drivers switched off the engines of their cars and got out, many wearing Nigerian robes which looked airy and comfortable in the sticky heat. They stood about chatting while vendors walked up and down peddling their wares, which included everything from Vicks cough drops to dustpans. There were even people at the side of the road with manual sewing machines, ready to do on-the-spot mending.

"Nigerian women are great businesspeople," Carlette told me, "and they are a force to be reckoned with. There are even women chiefs." I found that hard to imagine.

Once we were off the bridge and onto Ikoyi Island, it didn't take long to reach home, which was a house surrounded by trees and a garden. "No flowers, I'm afraid," sighed Carlette. "It's too hot for them. But the trees and bushes have exotic leaves which you can see from the veranda. I'll show you around tomorrow. Now let me take you to your room."

On the way upstairs Carlette explained to me the peculiarities of the house. "There is water only on the first floor," she said, "but you get used to that. We have a system which works very well." The shower had in it a wooden stool to sit on, an orange plastic bucket full of water, and a small blue one for dipping. Everything was bright and cheerful, just like Carlette.

That evening, in the living room, she said to me conspiratorially, "Do you realize that you and I are the first representatives of the women of Opus Dei here? I think that deserves a toast!" And she brought out drinks, and we toasted to the future work in Nigeria.

The following day, Father Gabiola came over to discuss with us the plans for my visit. He lived in Ibadan, where most of the apostolic work was going on, and he repeated what Fola Olumide had written: that the ladies were eager to meet a woman of Opus Dei. So we decided to include Ibadan in the itinerary. I had a ten-day visa.

Carlette drove me everywhere, even to early morning Mass. I visited the government secretarial college and a private one, and then had lunch at the state capitol with Victoria Gowon. I showed her brochures of Kianda and we discussed the possibility of a similar college in Lagos. "We need to raise the standard of efficiency, both in government offices and in the private sector," she said, "so a college of this kind would be welcome. However, you should speak to the Commissioner of Education. He will tell you how to go about it." And she made an appointment for me.

In Kenya we have inherited the British style of doing

things, and so I thought that on official visits it was proper to come straight to the point so as to waste as little as possible of the VIP's time. So when I was ushered into the Commissioner's office, I walked briskly the long length of red carpet that led to the enormous desk at which sat this imposing Nigerian gentleman dressed in traditional white robes and headdress. After the first greetings I opened my briefcase and began my story.

The Commissioner stopped me with a wave of his hand and, settling back in his chair, advised me in a fatherly fashion that I was going about things in a wrong way. "If you want to do anything in Nigeria," he said, "you must follow Nigerian customs. You have come from Kenya to visit Nigeria. I will ask how you like our country, how you left Kenya . . . I will offer you a soda . . . and after we have talked, then you may bring up your business."

I was very grateful for that lesson, one of the many I have learned on human relations from the refined ways of the African people. After the soda I showed him brochures of Kianda, and he seemed keen on the idea of a similar college in Lagos. "When do you plan to start? You will need to get registration . . ." I explained that this was just a preliminary visit, and he invited me to come again when my plans were better defined.

I flew by Nigerian Airlines to Ibadan, where I stayed at the Ibadan University guesthouse. Fola was there to welcome me. "I have invited the other ladies to my house tomorrow, and they are looking forward to meeting you," she said. "I'll come here to pick you up."

The following day, at Fola's house, the living room was full of Nigerian ladies in their glamorous national dresses. After the first introductions we had tea, and then they got down to the business of asking questions.

"You are the first woman of Opus Dei we have ever met," said Adeline Oseni. "How did you join?" I explained that I first encountered the Work in Ireland and became a member while I was still a student.

"What about married members?" asked Fola. "What do they do?"

"They are called supernumeraries, but the spirit is the same for all of us," I explained. "Each one tries to sanctify her work and do apostolate according to her personal state in life, single or married. They almost always live with their families and try to make their home a bright and cheerful place for their family and friends."

"Can I join, then?" she asked, looking very interested.

"There has to be a center first, with some women of Opus Dei to run it and teach the spirit of the Work."

I showed them slides of Kianda College and the other activities in Kenya, and they were very impressed. "When will there be something like that here?" asked Adeline. "Can't we start working now?"

"Yes," added Fola, "just write and tell us what we have to do and we'll do it." And the other ladies said the same. I told them how much the Father was praying for them and for the establishment of the women of Opus Dei in Nigeria.

Before leaving for Lagos I found a bulky package waiting for me in my room. It contained several decorated gourds, with a note from Adeline saying, "For the Father, from his Nigerian daughters."

When I arrived at Lagos Airport, Carlette and Pim were there, eager to hear how things had gone. "You must come back soon," Carlette said, "to get everything started." The following day, the Roeskes put me on the plane for home.

19

Lagoon College

Late at night the plane touched down at Jomo Kenyatta Airport, and I found Charo and Joan waiting for me, full of excitement, talking at the same time, saying, "How was the trip?" "What did you think of Nigeria?" "How is Carlette?" And then . . . "Olga, guess what? Both of us are going to Nigeria!"

So the work in Nigeria was really imminent. How happy the ladies would be! We talked excitedly in the car on the way home, and I learned that Father Robert Lozano was also leaving Kenya for Nigeria, to be Counsellor for that region.

During the coming months Charo and Joan got to know a number of Nigerian ladies through Gloria Olisemeka, who organized a garden party at the High Commissioner's residence to introduce them to people who could help. Fola and Adeline wrote from Ibadan, and Carlette from Lagos, "When are you coming again? You know you can always stay with us."

On May 17, 1972, Charo and I left for Lagos to lay the groundwork for the new college. We knew that it would be difficult, because Pim had warned me that things take a long time in Nigeria, and we didn't have that time. The men of Opus Dei had been there since 1966 and it was high time that we came to start the work with women.

As I gazed out the window of the plane carrying us to Lagos, I had a moment of panic. What were we two women going to do? Where would we start? What if we failed? I knew that the Father, as well as everyone we had left behind in Kenya, was praying for us, but how would things work out? I had no idea, and suddenly felt overwhelmed by the responsibility of it all. I turned to look at Charo, who gave me a serene, encouraging smile.

We were met by Carlette and Pim, who welcomed us and brought us to their home. After dinner we explained to them what we hoped to accomplish: "We have to register the college with the Ministry of Education and find premises for it where the women can live." Pim shook his head. "It takes ages to get papers through the Ministry," he said. "I know people who have waited for years and then given up."

The next morning, the Counsellor came over. He said, "You realize how important it is that this succeeds, don't you? Opus Dei is crippled without the women." He told us whom to contact in the Ministry of Education and warned us that negotiations take a long time. After that, we were on our own.

The Roeskes put their blue Volkswagen at our disposal, and we went out every morning for the early Mass. Afterwards we had breakfast with Carlette before starting on our work in town.

On the first day we met Mr. Badmos, the person in charge at the Ministry of Education. He explained that in order to be registered we had to present full information about the college, including the number and the credentials of staff members. Those who were not Nigerian would need work permits, but that was a matter for Immigration. For each step there was a paper to be signed and stamped by the person responsible, and only when all the papers were ready could we come back to him for registration. We left his office reeling at the thought of all that had to be done.

We were working on wheels within wheels. The proposed secretarial college had to have a name, a physical location, an ownership body or not-for-profit trust, a curriculum, a list of the names and credentials of its teachers, and work permits, and there were finances to be considered. Pim warned us not to be too optimistic.

Besides the slowness of the government machinery, there was also the problem that transactions in Nigeria were usually oiled with "dash" (a bribe, although Fola told me that many Nigerians interpreted it broadly as a traditional form of gift such as is given to a chief).

It was Pim who came up with the name for our college. We were talking about it after dinner one evening, and he said thoughtfully, "Lagos . . . lagoon . . . why don't you call it the Lagoon College?" Charo liked that, and so did I. From then on the college had a distinctive character and we could speak confidently of "the Lagoon Executive Secretarial College."

We worked out the curriculum and I telephoned Mercedes Morado, a director of Opus Dei in Rome, for details about the eight ladies who would be coming to start the Work in Nigeria with Charo and Joan.

From then on our days were spent in offices. Hour after hour we waited to see the person who had to approve our papers. At long last, when an approval seemed to be going through, an important government official died in England and the whole Ministry flew to London to accompany the body back to Nigeria for burial. A whole week was lost.

Meanwhile the priests had been searching for suitable premises to rent, and finally they discovered a new house on the mainland, in a residential area called Surulere. Charo and I went to look at it and we liked it, but before we could enter into a lease agreement we needed to have an ownership body. Again, the wheels within wheels.

"I'm sure the ladies in Ibadan will be able to help us," I told Charo. We traveled there one weekend, staying at the university guesthouse. In the university chapel a priest of the Work was giving a day of recollection for ladies, so Charo gave them a talk and afterwards we spoke to Fola about the ownership board. She understood at once. "I'll contact the others," she said, "and we'll meet you tomorrow afternoon at the guesthouse."

Half a dozen ladies turned up, including Adeline, and Charo and I told them what we had done so far and how we needed to set up a nonprofit body to rent the premises of the future Lagoon Executive Secretarial College. "Of course we can do that," said Adeline, speaking on behalf of all.

Fola added, "I sit on several architectural boards and I know the procedure. What shall we call it?" And then she suggested, "Why don't we call ours the Lagoon College Women's Executive Board?" Everyone approved, and she promised to start working on it right away.

Back in Lagos the round at the Ministry continued with the frustration of trying to get papers from one place to another, signed and stamped. Charo and I usually waited in the same office and observed the same people ambling in and out exchanging the news of the day, getting soft drinks from the fridge, and lamenting that the photocopier was broken. Occasionally someone cast a sympathetic glance in our direction, but on the whole we might as well have been part of the furniture.

Sitting in offices took up the whole working day, so it was four-thirty or five before we arrived home for lunch. We were hardly out of the car before Carlette was at the open door, smiling, eager to know how the day had gone. She looked after us like a mother and saw further than we guessed. One afternoon we came back dead tired and in low spirits; it seemed that nothing was moving. Then, as Charo swung the car into its place, Carlette came running out, beaming. "There's a surprise by your plate, a letter from Rome!" she exclaimed. We hurried in and found a letter from Mercedes, saying that the Father was praying very much for the work we were doing in Nigeria and for all the fruit that would come from it. That letter put new heart into us.

Sometimes Charo and I got on each other's nerves. There was so much tension, and each one reacted in a different way. One evening we were alone in the house and I went to bed while Charo let off steam playing "Moonlight Sonata" on the piano.

Carlette and Pim, realizing that we were coming to the end of our rope, gave us little surprises. One Saturday Carlette took us swimming. I can't recall where we got the swimsuits, but I do remember the sensation of drowning all my concerns in the clear, cool water of the pool. Another time Pim said in his quiet way, "These ladies need an outing," and they brought us to a hotel overlooking the sea, for a lovely dinner in a totally different environment. There was also the Sunday that they rented a motorboat and we all went across the lagoon to a beach on the opposite shore.

A time came when the premises had to be inspected and declared safe for a school. As the building was new and spacious, we expected this to be just a formality, but it wasn't. The first inspector walked several times around the house checking for fire hazards, and finally gave his verdict: "This house needs thirty-six fire extinguishers before it can be declared safe." "That's not possible," Charo said indignantly. "You're asking for more than four extinguishers per room!" But the inspector was adamant. He even told us where we had to buy them.

The second inspector declared the whole building to be unsafe because the windows and doors were wrongly positioned, and said they would have to be relocated before he could give his approval. This time the contractor was with us, and as Charo and I didn't react to hints about "dash," he took the inspector outside for a private conversation, and after that there were no more complaints about windows and doors.

Finally we got written permission to use the premises for a school. The curriculum and staff were also approved, and we presented our completed papers. Shortly afterwards Mr. Badmos called Charo and me into his office to give us our registration papers and to wish us all the best for the new school. The whole operation had taken two months.

Next we applied at the Immigration Office for the ten work permits, presenting a full report of the duly registered Lagoon College. After that we just had to wait for an answer; we had done all we could. So in July we returned home.

We told the Counsellor the outcome of our trip and asked him to pray that the work permits would be granted. "What will you do if they aren't?" he asked. I took a deep breath and answered, "We'll start all over again."

We didn't have to start all over again. In August Charo received a telephone call informing us that every one of the ten work permits had been granted! It was much more than we had dared hope for.

Charo and Joan left in November with the eight others (among whom were Florence Auma and Mary Mumbua) to start Lagoon College and the apostolates of the women of Opus Dei in Nigeria.

Carlette wrote to tell me that she and her husband had received a letter from the Father thanking them for all they had done to help get the Work started in Nigeria. That help continued until the Roeskes finally returned to Holland a few years later. They left their blue Volkswagen to Charo, for Lagoon College.

In December 1973 I met with the Father in Rome, and he told me how grateful he was for the way the Nigerians had opened their doors to us.

I was able to tell him about the girls' high school we were planning in Nairobi. The Father was very interested and asked what university they could go to afterwards. As the Royal Technical College had become Nairobi University in 1970, I said we would prepare our students to go there.

Then the Father said, "I'm going to give you the cornerstone for that school," and he gave me a chalice to bring back to Kenya.

20

The Father in Heaven

"Are all of you there?" It was the Counsellor calling. "We're coming over right now. We have something to tell you."

It was 7:15 P.M., June 26, 1975, and we were having dinner at Roshani, the Regional Advisory center. A few minutes later the priests arrived. "Let's go to the oratory," the Counsellor said, leading the way. We exchanged apprehensive glances as we filed into the pews. Nothing like this had ever happened before. Then the Counsellor went up beside the altar and after a moment's hesitation said in a shaking voice, "The Father passed away today."

There was a moment's silence, and then people began to sob. A cold numbness invaded me. The Father had left us, we would never see him again, I couldn't tell him anything anymore, he would no longer advise us . . . The Father was gone.

The priests led the prayers for the repose of the Father's soul and then left the oratory. Tere and I went after them to ask for more details. "What happened?" "Was he sick?" "What time did he die?" "Did he say anything?"

"I don't know anything more," the Counsellor murmured, and then he asked us to prepare everything for a Requiem Mass in the morning.

Cristina Cabello and Tere went out to the different centers to communicate in person the news that had left us shattered, while Ursula and I prepared the vestments for the following day's Mass. We put out all the feast-day things: the lace altar cloth, the pall with the seal of the Work embroidered in gold . . . I thought sadly of the one they were making at Kibondeni, with pearls and semi-precious stones, for the longed-for visit of the Father to Kenya. Now there could be no visit.

It was hard to tear ourselves away to bed that night. We stood around in the hall disconsolate, trying to imagine what was going on in Rome. "Isn't there anything we can do for the Father?" asked Tere. And then she said, "I know, we can send flowers!"

We sent seventy-three red roses—one for each year of the Father's life—together with my last words to the Father on earth: "For the Father, with all the affection and gratitude of his daughters in Kenya."

In the midst of his own grief, Don Alvaro wrote a long letter to the members of the Work about the last days our Father spent in this world.

On the morning of June 26 the Father had been in Castel Gandolfo, near Rome, with his daughters of the Roman College of Holy Mary. He said to them, "I will tell you, as I do whenever I come here, that you, by the simple fact of being Christians, have priestly souls. Your brothers who are laymen also have priestly souls. With your priestly soul and with God's grace, you can and should help the priestly ministry which we priests carry out. Together, we shall work effectively. I suppose that in everything you do . . . you find a reason to talk to God and to his Blessed Mother, who is our Mother, and to Saint Joseph, our father and lord, and to our guardian angels, so as to help this holy Church, our Mother, who is in such great need and who is having such a difficult time in the world these days. We should love the Church and the Pope very much. Ask our Lord to make our service of the Church and of the Pope effective."

After about twenty minutes the Father started feeling indisposed and the visit had to be brought to an end. He rested briefly and then returned to Rome, accompanied as usual by Don Alvaro del Portillo and Don Javier Echevarría. He looked happy and calm. On entering

Villa Tevere, a few minutes before noon, he went to greet our Lord in the tabernacle, pausing to make a deep genuflection accompanied by an act of love, as was his custom.

"Then," continued Don Alvaro, "we went up to the room where he usually worked, . . . and seconds after he had gone through the door he called out to Don Javier, 'Javi!'"

In that room there was a picture of Our Lady of Guadalupe which the Father always glanced at on entering. It received his last loving greeting, before he fell to the ground. God had granted his desire to die looking at a picture of Mary.

"For us," Don Alvaro wrote, "it was a sudden event. But for the Father, his death had undoubtedly been approaching—more in his soul, I would say, than in his body—because each day he more frequently offered his life for the Church."

On June 27 the Father was buried in the crypt of the Church of Our Lady of Peace. On the marble slab, under the seal of Opus Dei, were written two words summarizing his life: "EL PADRE." Beneath them were written the date of his birth, "9–I–1902," and that of his death, "26–VI–75."

From that moment on, his mortal remains have continuously been accompanied by prayers and expressions of gratitude from sons and daughters of his and from countless other people who have been drawn closer to God by the example and teaching of the founder of Opus Dei.

On June 29 we had a funeral Mass in the oratory of Kianda Residence. Relatives and friends of people of the Work came with their families, and the congregation overflowed into the corridor. The vestments the priest used were some that the Father had blessed in 1960 when we were coming to Kenya. Beside the altar there were big bouquets of gladioli and red roses.

After Mass people stayed around talking. When I thanked one of my friends for coming, she replied, "How could I not come? I've been helped by Opus Dei for years, and I owe everything to the Father."

A few days later, over a thousand people attended the funeral Mass at Holy Family Cathedral in Nairobi. And other Masses were celebrated in different parts of Kenya.

One of these was celebrated by Bishop Urbanus Kioko, "especially for his canonization, that it may be soon." In true African style, he challenged the youth with a story. "You young people, be generous with God!" he said. "Stop wasting your time thinking, 'Maybe I could do this or that, marry this one or that one.' Look, I'm going to tell you something. There was a donkey that was so hungry that he was at the point of death. A man saw this, took pity on him, and gave him two sweet potatoes. The donkey took them, delighted and grateful, and then began to think, 'Which of the sweet potatoes will I eat first? If I eat this one first, I'm sure that he'll take back the other. And if I eat the other first? The same. So what do I do? Which should I eat first?' Well, do you know what happened to the donkey? He died of starvation, with the two sweet potatoes untouched."

On September 15 Don Alvaro was unanimously elected the first successor of the founder of Opus Dei. Shortly afterwards the intercom rang out joyously with a message that had not been heard for three months: "The Father wants to see everyone by the staircase of La Montagnola!"

The whole household waited there, with a mixture of joy and sorrow, for the sanctuary door to open. In a few moments there would come through that door the Father—but it wouldn't be our founder. Yet when he appeared, visibly moved himself, I knew we really had a Father. "You have not elected Alvaro del Portillo," he said. "In electing the person who was longest beside our

Father, you have shown that you wanted to reelect our Father. The foundational period is over. We now begin the period of continuity."

After that I went to visit my parents, who were now living in London. After giving me a warm embrace, my father asked, "How did you do in Rome? Who is the new head of Opus Dei?" When I told him that Don Alvaro was now the Father, he nodded and said, "Of course. He was the one who had been longest beside the founder."

* 21 *

Kianda School

"Tazama, tazama, ni vema na vizuri ndugu kuisha pamoja kwa umoja . . ." (Look and see, it is right and fitting for brothers to live together in unity. . .).

So sang the school choir, accompanied by drums and *kayambas* (bamboo shakers), while sixty little nine-year-olds, wearing white T-shirts and colorful kangas, danced in two long lines onto the hockey field, leading the entrance procession for the solemn Mass of thanksgiving. Their silent, reverent movements formed an integrated unity glorifying God. They bent down, arms outstretched, and slowly raised them high to signify that God is the owner of heaven and earth, and their white-gloved hands fluttered like butterflies as they offered him glory. Kianda School was celebrating its twentieth anniversary.

The first three chaplains of the school concelebrated the Mass under a canopy before a congregation of nearly two thousand people, of all hues and creeds, seated on the hockey field bleachers. Many of them were alumnae of Kianda College and Kianda School, with their husbands and families.

I couldn't help but recall how it had all started. One day in 1973, Naomi Waiyaki, an alumna of Kianda College, said to me, "My daughter is in primary school now, but I would so much like for her to benefit from the personal attention given at Kianda, as I did. Couldn't you start a secondary school?" Other alumnae said the same. Later I mentioned this to the Father (Monsignor Escrivá), and he encouraged the idea.

In 1977 the first forty high-school students came. We put them at the back of the residence, far from the college and far from the residents. But despite our best efforts, a teacher would sometimes bump into an impish teenager skidding gleefully along the waxed corridor near the main entrance. We realized that this was only the beginning and that sooner or later they would take over Kianda.

By 1987 it became necessary to have a primary section from which we could recruit students for the high school. The first batch of six-year-olds arrived on the scene in 1989 and started a permanent livening of the whole place with their skipping and chirping and great zest for life.

To run the school we got Margaret Roche to come from Kenya High School. Margaret is Irish and came to Kenya in 1969, soon after graduating from Galway University. She taught in several Nairobi schools, including Kenya High, which by then was very different from what it had been in 1960, largely in that it was now almost entirely African. Margaret came into contact with the Work while teaching there.

Margaret is still the principal of Kianda School. Assisting her is Mary Kibera, an alumna of Kianda College who went on to Nairobi University, where she earned degrees in French and education. She joined the Work while a resident at Kianda. The scientist of the trio running the school is Lina Sequeira, a Goan lady who came into contact with the Work while studying at Nairobi University . . .

Margaret Roche, flushed and visibly moved, gave the introduction:

> We are starting this celebration with a Mass to thank God for Kianda and for the founder of Opus Dei, who made it possible. Twenty years ago he gave Olga Marlin the cornerstone for this school, the chalice which is being used for today's Mass.
>
> Olga, Tere Temes, and Cuca Canel are among the valiant group of women who first came to this

compound over thirty-five years ago, when it was only one small cottage and acres of waving grass. They had a vision of education as a way of preparing our women for life's challenges. In a way, Kianda today is a culmination of those dreams.

As all of you gathered here know, the principle on which Kianda School functions is the close relationship between parents, teachers, and students. It was the founder of Opus Dei who taught us that the most important people in a school are the parents, followed by the teachers, and then the students.

The crowds filling the hockey field were all very quiet and attentive throughout the service.

After the Mass, the chairperson of the Kianda Past Students' Association, Ann Muigai, spoke about what Kianda meant to her. She was one of the first students of the school and is now a supernumerary of Opus Dei. Ann is a professor of molecular biology at Jomo Kenyatta University; she is, in fact, head of the department and is the youngest member of the university senate. Married with two children, she is studying for her Ph.D.

"I'm proud to be a Kianda graduate," she began, and everyone clapped. "What I appreciate most about this school is the training we were given. We were helped to grow in self-confidence, through the tutorials and activities like drama and public speaking.

"Each one was treated as an individual and encouraged to be herself. We learned to be independent, to do things because we wanted to, not because we were forced. All this helped me very much later on in my university career.

"You don't know what it's like out there until you leave school. You get used to being treated as a person and it's a shock when you find that at college nobody cares. You meet with a lot of indifference. We Kianda alumnae want to help change that."

The traditional and modern dances that followed had been choreographed by the girls themselves. When the entertainment was over, people were reluctant to go and stood around chatting and renewing old acquaintances. I found it difficult to maneuver my way around in the throng of people.

Maureen Mboya, now Mrs. Odero, came over to greet me, accompanied by her daughters, Diana and Nancy, who are both in Kianda School. "Aunty Olga," she said, "Diana is making her First Communion next Sunday. Will you be able to come?" As I promised to be there, I vividly recalled the circumstances surrounding Maureen's First Communion many years before.

Then Cuca called me over to greet Eva Beauttah, one of the first students in the secretarial college. "Imagine," Cuca said, taking me by the arm, "I no longer feel like the mother of the students, but the grandmother! Eva is here with her daughter Ella and her granddaughter Maysara, who's already in first grade. Three generations of Kianda students!"

Eva, who is a supernumerary, gave me a big hug. "It's a proud day for Kianda parents," she said. "Do you remember the interview Margaret and Mary Kibera had on television in 1976, before the school started? They explained the advantages of a day school—the importance of children being at home with their families and of parents having personal contact with their daughters. Most parents wanted to send their children to boarding schools.

"Now it's the other way around. They're trying to take them out. Parents are realizing that they lose their children in boarding schools. They don't know what's going on. The children are educated by their peers, and if the values of the peers are different from those of the parents, they lose their parents' values."

One of the fathers overheard this and came up to us. "One of the things I found hardest," he said, "was the number of meetings I had to attend at this school. But now I realize that this greater commitment pays off. We now come to the school out of interest in the education of our children—not just to find out their grades. We are participants, not just spectators."

As the student population grew from year to year, so did the need for classrooms, lab facilities, and transportation. The parents were asked to help the Kianda Foundation raise funds, and they readily did so. The result was another two-story cream-colored building with red-tiled roof and open veranda, built at the front of the Kianda compound, with four labs, eight classrooms, and home economics and staff rooms.

Lina Sequeira teaches biology. Before coming to Kianda she worked as a research scientist with Dr. Thomas Odhiambo at the International Center of Insect Physiology and Ecology. I first met her when she was still a student at Nairobi University.

"We live in a very competitive society," she said to me, "and without paper credentials you don't get far. It's a pity, because sometimes there is so much pressure for good grades that the children don't have time to enjoy what they're learning. Everyone is beginning to realize that a more human education is needed. Children are not machines. They have to have space to develop virtues while they work.

"People are hungry for education. I don't know of any other country where the national examinations make headlines every year. The whole country turns around them, teachers squirm, children sweat with fear, while politicians apportion blame."

"Are you happy with Kianda's results?" I asked.

"Yes," she replied, "especially considering that we are a girls' day school. In 1982, when we took the national exams for the first time, our name didn't appear on the lists, and this year we came in second in the nation. The Minister of Education, Mr. Joseph Kamotho, told parents to think about sending their children to day schools near their homes because those day schools can also make it 'like Kianda.'"

Mary Kibera is the soul of the tutorial department. Her main interest there is in family development, because of the effect the family has on character building and on the future stability of the children. Since the majority of the Kianda parents are young (most of the children being in the primary section), Mary sees the importance of teaching the skills of parenting, of creating families where values are taught and lived. In this she is helped by the older parents in the school. Having been through the same problems, they are able to advise the younger ones.

In the words of a great educator and father of a family, Tomás Alvira, who was also the first supernumerary of Opus Dei, "Each one of our children is a very complex being, with a wealth of facets, but forming a unity. Educators can never forget this. We parents should be interested in the education of our children at home and in the school. We have to find time for our family, but it is also important that we find some time, even if only a little, to dedicate to our children's school, to help it function better, which in the end is to help our children, the aim we parents should set for ourselves."

It was evening when the last car rolled away, people waving from the windows.

We were standing at the spot where it had all begun. There was the old cottage—now dwarfed by the new buildings, but still retaining its charm. I remembered our first African student, thirty-six years ago, walking to school with her shoes in a bag, determined to improve her life and that of her family. So many other girls followed in her footsteps, and today, for their daughters, education is not the bitter struggle it was for them. Now women like Ann Muigai are not only heading departments but also pursuing Ph.D.'s, and living out their calling to Opus Dei as mothers and as professionals.

I remembered what Blessed Josemaría had told us before we came to Kenya: that "when we begin our work in a country, we cannot isolate ourselves, but must form roots in it," and that our role was to be like the stick that is placed beside a young tree to help it grow straight and strong—that the deepest work would be done by the people we formed who were from that country.

I realized that the sapling had grown into a sturdy tree.

22

The University of Navarre Clinic

Dr. Batey put down the X rays, sat back in his chair, and looked hard at me. "You have a lousy spine," he said at last. "You better treat it like glass."

Ever since Easter of 1975 (the year Blessed Josemaría Escrivá went to heaven), when my back locked while I was sitting forward in a chair and painting Easter eggs, it had become increasingly painful. On my return from London in September I went to see Dr. Batey; he ordered X rays, and this was the result.

I didn't know how to deal with a "glass" back, and by November it reached such a stage that surgery was advised. I was admitted to Nairobi Hospital for a laminectomy and discharged a couple of weeks later, after being cautioned to rest for a while. However, after two months my back still didn't feel right, so the surgeon recommended a few days at the coast.

Cuca and Pilu accompanied me to Mombasa, where we walked and swam, but the pain continued. The plane trip home was torture. I felt as if a dentist's drill was being run up my spine. After that I was confined to bed for two weeks, unable to put my right foot down. Finally one morning Tere helped me into the car and drove me carefully back to the surgeon's office. On the way she blurted out, "I hope you don't need another operation!" That horrifying possibility had never crossed my mind, but it turned out to be the case. In February 1976 I had a second laminectomy.

After that, months passed and I didn't seem to be able to recover. Tere brought me to Dr. Batey, who recommended that I see a specialist in London. On the way home Tere said, "Why don't you call your father? Your sister is a doctor there, and I'm sure she would know what to do."

She helped me dial the number, and we both waited in suspense while the phone rang. My father answered it. "Daddy?" I said. I was weak and my voice shook as I imagined his comforting presence and strength, which held out hope for me in my helpless physical condition. "My back is bad and I have to see a specialist in London!" There was a moment's silence, and then Daddy called out sternly, his voice trembling and his New York accent even more pronounced than usual, "You come home right away, you hear me?" With Tere beside me I shed tears of comfort and relief. I had been out of commission for a long time.

While Tere organized the trip, my father spoke with my sister Liz, and she arranged for a specialist friend of hers to see me as soon as I arrived. Virginia Camp, the specialist, shook her head over the amount of bone that had been removed, and immediately booked me into a rehab facility called Farnham Park, in Slough. It was within commuting distance from Woodlands, an Opus Dei center in Ealing, so I lived in the rehab facility five days a week, coming to Woodlands for the weekend.

Formerly a stately home, Farnham Park stood on ample grounds which now contained sports fields, a running track, a carpentry workshop, workout rooms, a gym . . . Many of the patients were football players with dislocated joints. There was a policeman who had hurt his back flinging a thief over a wall. Several women were recovering from bone surgery.

It was a new experience for me. The efficient British nurses wore starched white uniforms and had a brisk no-nonsense manner. On the first day I hesitantly got into the admissions line, and after being put through the formalities by one of the formidable nurses, I was shown around by a kindly social worker. I felt bewildered by everything. In the workshops patients were busily making all sorts of things, and my guide told me cheerily, "Tomorrow you will start working in the carpentry shop." I recoiled at the prospect, knowing nothing about carpentry, but she pretended not to notice.

I soon got into my routine, which was heat treatment under a lamp, followed by easy exercises and then long periods of time in the carpentry room, standing at the tallest table, working on different projects. The day's schedule at Farnham Park was tight, so there wasn't much time for socializing except at mealtimes and the morning and afternoon tea breaks. One day I struck up a conversation with a kindly woman named "Chippy" Green. I found out that she too was interested in education. Her field was remedial teaching. She helped disadvantaged youngsters integrate into the normal system. For Chippy there were no hopeless cases, and she had succeeded in setting many youngsters on their feet, sometimes in original ways. She kept horses, and one way that her students came to life was by relating to a horse—and then to Chippy. We talked a lot about our teaching experiences in Greater London and in Kenya.

Chippy was a Methodist, and I could tell that she had a constant awareness of God, so one day I asked her a favor. At Farnham Park I wasn't able to go out for Mass, but the parish priest kindly agreed to come and give me Holy Communion whenever he could. As I was the only Catholic patient and the Irish nurse wasn't available to accompany me the first day he came, I asked Chippy if she would do so. She said yes, and in one of the visiting rooms I received Communion, Chippy sitting behind me. The next time, I hesitated to ask her again, but she approached me, saying, "May I have the privilege of accompanying you again when you receive Communion?"

As my health improved, so did my appreciation of Farnham Park and its staff. The place no longer seemed so gloomy, nor the nurses so formidable, and I really enjoyed the carpentry work, gradually working my way down to the lowest table. (The tables were graded in height to allow for gradually increasing flexion of the back.) By the end of my stay I had made everything there was to be made, as well as some extras like a trestle for Lena Fernández's vestment-making workshop at Woodlands. As this was a bit complicated, some of the other patients lent a hand.

I also found instructions for making a little wooden donkey with cart, and set about making one as a present for the Father. When I had been at Farnham Park for two months, my back was strong again, muscles compensating for lost bone. In fact, I had acquired so much strength in my muscles that I became dangerous to have around. At Woodlands I shut off the shower faucet so tightly that no one could shower there until I returned the following weekend and loosened it. I also closed the inkpot so tightly that no one was able to use it anymore.

By the time Farnham Park pronounced me fit to return home, I was raring to go. I could imagine the amount of work everyone had, and also I had received a touching letter from Tere. "The news that you are well and will soon be coming home," she said, "arrived in the middle of a power failure, which is just as well, because my tears of joy passed unnoticed."

For ten years my back held out very well, with me doing my exercises faithfully every day, but then it started feeling like something was loose. One day I realized for the first time that my spine seemed to be swiveling at the waist, as if I were in two pieces. It was a very strange sensation.

Dr. Batey sent me for more X rays, and Conchita and I went to find out the results. My condition was bad and the doctor did not hide it. "You are suffering," he said, "from subluxation of the spine. In other words, the lower part of the spine has collapsed. I'm afraid you may have to resign yourself to a future in a wheelchair." I looked at him horror-struck. "What do I do now?" "Go home and lie flat. The less you move that back, the better." I was stunned and on the way home couldn't respond to Conchita's encouraging "You'll see, it won't be as bad as all that . . ."

While I lay in bed, the rest of the family got busy. "We're considering what to do," Tere told me, "because you must see a specialist. You could go back to London. On the other hand, Father James Planell has a friend who is a well-known trauma specialist and works in the clinic of the University of Navarre. How would you like to go there?" I had often heard about the clinic attached to the medical school of the University of Navarre, a corporate undertaking of Opus Dei in Spain. There I would receive spiritual as well as medical care. "I would like to go to the clinic," I said.

The specialist, Dr. José Cañadell, was ready to see me, so everything was arranged for me to go as soon as possible. Dr. Batey insisted that I travel as an invalid, accompanied by Conchita, using wheelchairs throughout and taking the heavy doses of drugs he prescribed. I was ready to do anything to ward off the specter of a future in a wheelchair.

It was a long and tiring journey, but between the drugs and Conchita I made it to Pamplona Airport in one piece and was wheeled through the door, feeling very invalidish. My first surprise was to find waiting for us a Spanish epitome of an English nurse. She took immediate control of everything. With the help of the driver, she settled me in the front seat of the taxi and rode with us to the clinic. She was Carmen López, a member of Opus Dei whom Conchita had met before. They talked animatedly, but I realized that all the while, Carmen was keeping a clinical and very compassionate eye on me.

At the entrance to the clinic I was bundled into a wheelchair and taken with Conchita to a reception room.

Carmen told us to wait there, and then she hurried off. After what seemed a very long time, she came back to say that there was a shortage of beds, so I would spend the first night on the second floor, before moving to the fifth. "What about Conchita?" I asked. "Oh," she said, "don't worry. Every room has an armchair that is convertible into a bed for a relative or companion of the patient." I was very grateful for that. The room was homey. In fact, the whole clinic had the family atmosphere of a center of the Work.

No time was wasted. That same evening, a hefty young doctor in immaculate white coat came to examine me. I stood facing the wall and he began to pummel my spine, starting at the neck. When he reached my waist, I saw a thousand stars and yelled, at which he apologetically ceased his exploration. After that there was the taking of X rays of the back, from every possible position. Occasionally one of the radiologists asked, "Were you involved in an accident?" I felt very apprehensive.

Next day the specialist, Dr. Cañadell, came to see me, X rays in hand. Pulling up a chair, he sat near the head of my bed and explained exactly what was happening to my spine. The technical details were lost on me, but I really didn't care; all I wanted was to get better. When he had finished, I turned to him and asked tremulously, "Can you save me?" There was a short pause, and then in the kindest possible way he slid his arm along the head of the bed and, bending near me, said firmly, "You are already saved." Waves of relief flowed over me, and I felt boundless confidence in Dr. Cañadell. He explained that he would have to operate and insert Harrington rods to support the spine, which was fine by me. He knew what he was doing.

The operation took place a couple of days later, on February 22. For three weeks I lay immobile in bed, and had ample time to observe what was going on around me. Every morning a team of cleaning women arrived, dressed in spotless pink and white uniforms, pushing a closed white cart that held all kinds of cleaning implements. I don't know how they managed this, but there was never any smell of detergent, even in the bathroom, and yet this clinic has the lowest rate of infection in all of Europe.

The white hospital gown I was wearing had a feminine touch, a little lace border around the neckline, and I commented on it to Carmen. "That is the work of the women who look after the services of the clinic," she said. "They are always thinking up new details to make illness more bearable and to personalize the care of the patients. We told them that the male patients felt uncomfortable in the white hospital gown, so they designed for them a beige one with a V neck, a dark brown bias binding, and a fake pocket with the initials 'CUN' in dark brown. It looks like a pajama top. The service department is the heart of the clinic; it's what gives it the unique family atmosphere that sets it apart. Blessed Josemaría declared in no uncertain terms that the clinic would not start without the service department."

There was a chapel in the clinic and a chaplain assigned to each floor, so I could go to confession whenever I wanted and receive Holy Communion every day. The Sunday Mass was transmitted on the closed-circuit TV and I could follow it from my bed.

Orderlies in whites moved the patients from place to place in wheelchairs or on stretchers. They were strong, kind men, as I discovered when they had to transfer me from bed to stretcher and take me to the X-ray department. They handled me as gently as if I were a baby and moved the stretcher carefully so that I wouldn't feel any bumps, all the while making comforting conversation and greeting colleagues who passed by. I learned that many of the orderlies and maintenance men were in the Work.

When three weeks had passed, the hefty young doctor

came to visit me. He worked on Dr. Cañadell's team, so I had seen him quite often since that first pummeling. After clearing his throat a couple of times, he took up his position, hands behind back, and presented me with the hypothetical case of a person in my condition whose back had been firmly braced but later gave trouble because it was weak in front . . . It was a gentle introduction to my next visit from Dr. Cañadell, in which he explained that a second operation was needed to consolidate the spine from the front. That wasn't easy to accept, but I had no choice.

The operation was set for March 19, but later Dr. Cañadell postponed it to the twentieth "so you can enjoy Saint Joseph's Day in peace." On that feast day the nurse brought in for Conchita and me a beautifully presented tray with drinks and appetizers, and then a special dinner. We celebrated, but I feared that second operation because I realized it would be a delicate one, and also because I had scarcely recovered from the first one.

The following day Carmen came down with me to the operating room and then said casually, "By the way, don't worry if you find yourself in the ICU when you wake up. It's just a precaution." I was properly scared. But when they wheeled the stretcher onto the platform in the brightly lit operating room and it clicked into place, I suddenly recognized in front of me the kindly eyes of Dr. Cañadell behind the green mask, and felt reassured.

When I awoke I was not in the ICU. A nurse was speaking to me gently, and next thing I knew I was back in my room, surrounded by tubes and bottles and with Conchita beside me. A few days later the tubes and bottles were removed and it was now a matter of lying in bed until I recovered. Conchita stayed long enough to see that I would be all right, and then she returned to Kenya.

My parents came from London to visit me and were very impressed by everything. They commented on the decor—the pictures and lamps and comfortable furniture that made cozy corners in the corridors. "There is a team of decorators," Carmen explained, "and they upholster the furniture themselves. Other items are contributed by Opus Dei cooperators and friends." "It's so different from any other hospital I've seen," Mother said. "They're usually so white and sterile." And to me she commented, "Everyone is treated as an important *person* here. The receptionists, cleaners, and workmen are respected as much as the doctors."

Dr. Cañadell invited my parents for lunch and then showed them around the university. Mother told me how impressed my father was. "He is immensely grateful to the doctor and wanted to give him a present," she said, "but Dr. Cañadell would only accept a contribution towards the new chapel they are building for the clinic. Of course Daddy gave it and thanked him from his heart."

Another day my father asked Dr. Cañadell if they could see the X rays. The doctor had the X rays brought in and then held them up against the light, explaining everything he had done. My father asked, "May I have a set to show to my doctor daughter in London?" I felt embarrassed, thinking it was not the thing to do to ask an eminent doctor to give over his work to be scrutinized by another doctor. However, Dr. Cañadell didn't hesitate for a moment. "Of course," he said. Daddy really appreciated that. Mother told me that the visit to the clinic had greatly increased his understanding of Opus Dei, and that he told her he was very happy that I was part of it.

Mother was in the room when I stood for the first time after all those weeks. The nurses had been preparing me by raising the bed a little each day, and finally a day came when the doctor said I could get out of bed. I was given some drops to prevent dizziness, and then Dr. Cañadell came in with his whole team. He sat in a chair to watch the proceedings, while Mother looked on. Getting my feet on the ground was a slow, painstaking effort requiring plenty of assistance, but at last it was done, and I exclaimed triumphantly, "I feel taller!" I turned to Dr. Cañadell, who was discreetly wiping his eyes, and then I took a couple of steps to look out the window. I couldn't remain standing for long because of the pain, so I was put back to bed. Mother was touched at how the doctor and his team had come to watch me "like a family hovering over the baby's first steps."

A plastic corset was made to measure, and encased in this I could begin the slow process of learning to walk again. Meeting with encouraging smiles from the staff, I pushed my walker around the corridors of the clinic, rhythmically repeating to myself Carmen's strict instructions on how to go about it: "firm, slow, sure." I felt like the Little Mermaid, whose legs were like swords. It depressed me to see how little progress I was making, and one afternoon Carmen found me in tears.

Early the next morning she came into my room, brisk and purposeful. "You're coming home now," she said, "so let's see how we manage." "What?" I exclaimed, in surprise and consternation. "Yes, I've spoken to Dr. Cañadell and he says that if we take every precaution you can come home." Home was Mendilaz, the center where Carmen lived.

In the novelty and fuss of leaving the clinic, I forgot all about my discouragement. The move to Mendilaz marked my change from invalid to convalescent.

After several months at Mendilaz—a time brightened by the care and thoughtfulness of Carmen and the others at the center, as well as a visit from Chippy and her husband and one from Mother and Brigid—at the end of September I made another visit to Dr. Cañadell, and he declared me fit to go home, provided I continued to wear the corset for some time.

So by the first of October I was home again. Eight

months before, on the way to the airport, Pilu had speculated on how long I might be away. I hadn't dared hazard a guess . . .

I visited Dr. Batey in his office to show him the work Dr. Cañadell had done, and he was amazed. He examined the scars, watched me walk, had me bend as far as I could, and exclaimed over everything. At that time Dr. Batey already had cancer, and shortly afterwards he died in his native Scotland. I was deeply impressed that being so ill himself, he was able to take such interest in me and rejoice with me at my recovery.

23

Fanusi Study Center

One of the more disconcerting events in Nairobi is to walk into a university students' riot, or worse, to drive into one. The frenzied students block roads, stone motorists, burn cars, and generally wreak havoc in the neighborhood. Yet a university, with the highly trained workforce it produces, is essential to any country.

When the university started, in 1970, it was easy to get admitted to it, provided one had good grades. The government had encouraged everyone who could to go on with their studies, and university education was free, including textbooks and room and board. The government even provided pocket money. Nevertheless, women students were still a small minority.

While in Rome in 1973, I had told Monsignor Escrivá about the high school we wanted to start at Kianda. He liked the idea, but immediately asked, "Will the girls be able to go on to college?" I was struck that he thought so far ahead, but assured him that they would be able to go to Nairobi University.

However, by the time the first Kianda high-school students had graduated in 1982 and were ready to go to college, things had changed dramatically. The student population had multiplied over the years and the dorms were overflowing. The lecture halls were so packed that some students had to listen from outside and take notes on their knees.

The government could no longer afford to pay for their education, and, little by little, privileges that the undergraduates had come to consider rights were being withdrawn. No longer were they given "boom" (pocket money), basic food (a plate of porridge or of beans and corn), or free textbooks, and eventually there was a "cost sharing" of tuition with parents.

Then came the riots. They started as a student reaction to the brutal murder of a popular Kikuyu politician, J. M. Kariuki, and included stone throwing, overturning of cars, and vandalism. The students were set upon by the city police and by the much-feared riot police, which led to injuries and arrests and then a closing of the university for an indefinite period. The students tended to consider themselves an elite (the people with brains who had "made it"), not realizing that they had a responsibility to put their talents to the service of others.

Some of the female students applied to Kianda Residence to escape from the chaos. At first we could admit them, but as the primary school was constantly expanding, one floor after another being converted into classrooms, we realized we would have to find another location.

We wanted to provide a residence and study center for university women, a kind of haven where they could study in peace and safety. It was a crying need. With more and more girls finishing high school and entering the university, the women's dorms could no longer accommodate them all, and they were given an allowance to pay for alternatives.

Some of them attended the monthly days of recollection at Kianda, although it was quite far away. "Why don't you get a place near here?" Lina Sequeira shyly asked me one day. "We're still building up the school," I explained, shaking my head. But Lina insisted. "Look at that plot across the road," she said. "It's all bush. There's nothing on it but an old tin house on stilts, where nobody can be living."

Tere, Cuca, and I discussed the situation.

"We have to continue admitting the students," Tere insisted. "In the residence we can help them grow in that maturity they must transmit to others. Today's students are tomorrow's leaders. They will be the ones who influence society and provide role models for Kenyan women in the future."

I said, "You know what Brigitte told me? 'I wish you could take more students in the residence. We learn so much here, and I think others should be given that chance.' I asked her what she meant, and she said that at Kianda she has learned to live a disciplined life, to study hard, and to help other people."

"In other words, she's learning to use her freedom responsibly," concluded Tere, "instead of attempting to solve problems by rioting, breaking windows, and burning cars."

The Father (Don Alvaro) was concerned about the university because, as he put it during one of our get-togethers, "a university must play a primary role in contributing to human progress. Since the problems facing humanity are multiple and complex (spiritual, cultural, social, economic, etc.), university education must cover all these aspects." He felt strongly that a desire to work for the common good is not enough; that the way to make it effective is to prepare capable men and women who can pass on to others the maturity they themselves have acquired.

"We have to get a place near the university for a women's residence and cultural center," we said to one another. "They badly need a library, because in the university library there isn't enough room to read, there aren't enough books to go around . . ." We discussed the matter endlessly.

"Let's think about the place Lina suggested," Cuca said. "That plot would be ideal."

"I don't know," I said doubtfully. "It's on the campus, so it probably belongs to the university. But I can ask the advice of my friend Damaris Ayodo. Her husband is a member of the Cabinet, and they live near the women's dorms."

Damaris told me what she knew. "Most of the properties around here are government-owned and are occupied by civil servants." Then she added, "If you can find an empty, undeveloped plot, perhaps the government would consider giving it to you for a university center and residence, because the education of women is a priority."

Tere and Cuca began the search for a government property, and it took them to the Registrar of Lands, the Commissioner of Lands, and the Survey of Kenya. An alumna of Kianda College worked in the Survey office, and she helped them identify possible plots. We applied to the Registrar in writing, listing the plots and asking about them, and received a reply saying that all of these were already allocated, but that we might want to look at Plot No. 10. We looked it up in the Survey . . . it was the one near the women's dorms!

The Minister of Lands, Mr. G. G. Kariuki, had a daughter attending Kianda School, so we asked his advice. He told us to write an official letter from the Kianda Foundation to the Ministry requesting that plot for the purpose of putting up a cultural center and residence for university women. We did that, and then waited and prayed.

A day came when the official brown envelope appeared on my desk. "Tere, it's come!" I cried, waving the envelope. "What's come?" she asked. "The letter from the Ministry of Lands," I said. "I don't dare open it . . ."

We looked at the envelope in suspense for a few moments before I slit it open. Dated November 16, 1979, the letter informed us that our request was granted. We read and reread it to make sure we had understood properly . . . We had!

Now that we had a plot of land, the local contribution to our project, we could start raising funds for the building. We submitted a brief to the Architects & Engineers Collaborative and asked them to draw up the blueprints.

We decided to call the university center "Fanusi." This is the Swahili word for the kind of lantern that hangs at the back of the dhows that ply the Indian Ocean; they act as guides for those coming behind. On one of her shopping expeditions in town, Sol found a brass fanusi and brought it home. "The first decoration for the new building!" she said exultantly.

It was difficult to raise funds for a university center, and in 1983 the project was still stuck. Tere, who had cut an "F" out of silver paper and glued it to a prayer card of our Father that she kept on her desk, was desperate.

"No one wants to support a project for university students," she lamented. "Look at this pile of refusals. It's so shortsighted. These are the women who will give themselves to others in the future through their professional work and social and philanthropic activities. They are the ones who will change the country."

I wrote to my father about our financial difficulties, and he offered to advise me if I wanted to fundraise in the United States. So my turn came to travel in search of money. On September 17, 1983, I set out on a journey that would take me to England, the United States, and Canada.

The first stop was London, where Daddy went over the material we had prepared. To my surprise, he frowned on it. "This is much too small a project," he said. "No one will take it seriously. Do you really expect to build a university center with the amount you're asking for here?"

"No," I answered, "it's just the first phase."

"Then include all the phases. If you fundraise in America, you fundraise for a million."

With the help of Anne Dickensen, an architect who was staying with me at Dawliffe Hall, an Opus Dei center in Chelsea, we reconstructed the whole Fanusi and revised the memorandum accordingly. Then we prepared a dozen dossiers for prospective donors. After approving the work we had done, Daddy said, "I want to buy you some clothes. To get a million you have to look like a million," and he bought me a beautiful maroon suit.

While I was with my parents in Berkhamsted, Chippy Green came to take me to dinner at their home in the nearby village of Harpenden. She knew why I had come to London, and as we drove along I told her more about Fanusi and our plans for university women. I asked her to pray for the success of the fundraising.

Before we reached the village, Chippy suddenly pulled the car to the side of the road, opened her handbag, and drew out a thick envelope which she shyly put into my hand, saying, "This will be a start for you, love."

Fortified by my father's help and Chippy's solidarity with us, I boarded the British Airways plane for New York.

When I came out of the airport in New York, Joan McIntosh and Dorothy Maloney were waiting for me. Everything looked neat and tidy in the September sunshine, and I noticed a general air of prosperity. On the way home in the car, they filled me in on the latest news.

"We had a get-together at Hunter College for members, cooperators, and friends of the Work," said Dorothy. "Father Joseph Muzquiz was there, and he was very moved. He and Father Sal came to the United States in 1948 to start Opus Dei in this country. They were two then, and at this get-together Father Joseph saw over a thousand people." Father Joseph was one of the first three priests of Opus Dei, the other two being Father José María Hernández de Garnica and Don Alvaro del Portillo.

I soon settled in and began following up the leads I had been given. I spent hours by the phone, looking up numbers and making appointments. In the end I made thirty-five visits, in New York City, Philadelphia,

Chicago, Ottawa, and D.C. I spoke on the phone with Elise Rockart, the teacher from Boston who had once made such an impact on our Kianda students, and she was enthusiastic about Fanusi and discovered a private foundation that promised to help with the financing.

People in the United States were curious to know more about the political situation in Kenya, which they felt was too dictatorial. I tried to explain what is meant by Kenya's "one-party democracy." Although it sounds like a contradiction in terms, "one-party democracy" reflects the traditional method of government, by which government was vested unquestioningly in the Elders and transferred only at their death. Although things are changing, authority still wields a strong hold on the citizens of Kenya. The people I talked to found this almost impossible to understand.

My brother Randal arranged a visit for me to Ottawa so that I could present my project to the Canadian Overseas Development Agency and spend a weekend with his family. He and Elaine now had five children, ranging in age from two to twelve. Randal was a philosophy professor at Carleton University, and his family reminded me very much of our own.

A few days later, as I was visiting a childhood friend, Lois Dean, in D.C., she told me that one day she had seen a taxi pull up in front of our old house. A tall man had gotten out, stood for a while gazing at the house, and then crouched down to get a child's eye view of the place with his camera. She guessed it must have been one of us, and it turned out to be Randal. I could understand him. It is a strange experience to visit places that continue to exist when the persons who gave them life for you are no longer there.

The visit that was decisive for Fanusi took place in the Empire State Building, a magical place for me with its childhood associations ("as high as . . . the Empire State Building!"), and the result was magical. With a stroke of his wand (a couple of phone calls), Mr. Robinson, the representative of a Dutch foundation, paved the way for the funding of the university study center.

Tired and happy, I left for Rome, where I had the privilege of meeting with the Father, who asked with interest about my parents and my travels. I told him what a joy it had been to meet so many people of the Work in the different centers where I had stayed, and how happy they all were with his recent visit. I could see that the Father was touched, but he simply said, "We are a family." Then he gave me his blessing for everyone in Kenya and I returned home.

Fanusi opened in 1987, and ever since, its directors have tried to realize the ideal set forth by Monsignor Escrivá: "A university must educate its students to have a sense of service to society, promoting the common good with their professional work and their activity. University people should be responsible citizens with a healthy concern for the problems of other people and a generous spirit which brings them to face these problems and to resolve them in the best possible way. It is the task of the universities to foster these attitudes in their students" (*Conversations with Monsignor Escrivá*, no. 74).

The rural projects carried out during summer vacations have proved one of the most effective means for doing this. Groups of students spend a week or ten days in remote villages, teaching the women and girls from their own store of knowledge. The experience is always an eye-opener for the students, who generally return saying they learned much more than they taught.

"The people have nothing, yet they are so happy," said an art student who had taught adult literacy. "The tea pickers were delighted because now they can write their names instead of putting a thumbprint on the receipts."

"The little I could teach them meant so much to the women," a law student commented. "I explained about land ownership, title deeds, and women's rights, and they suddenly realized they can have some security."

A medical student who had helped out in a dispensary couldn't get over the experience. "I saw so much silent suffering," she said. "The people even thanked me for the little I did."

Lucy Wanjiru told the director, "In the residence I have grown academically and spiritually. I have had so many opportunities that others haven't had, and it has made me realize that I've got to study hard so that in the future I can be of service to God and to others."

Fanusi today is a hive of activities. It is overflowing with residents and in urgent need of expansion.

24

Kenyan Elders

"He's got the whole world in his hands. . . . He's got Kenya in his hands!" chorused the Kianda girls enthusiastically, clapping and swaying as they sang. We were in the school auditorium rehearsing for the arrival of Pope John Paul II on May 6, 1980, his first visit to our country. The school children were to welcome him at the airport with banners, flags, and songs.

"Merche has been asked to set up the flowers at Holy Family Cathedral, where the Pope will go after he leaves the airport. Margaret Khamisi is going to help her . . ." "How lucky they are! They won't need cards . . ." Everyone was trying to get invitation cards for the different events which would take place during the Holy Father's three-day visit to Nairobi.

"Perhaps Pamela Mboya can get me some," I said. "As a representative to the United Nations, she is sure to have invitations."

Much to my surprise, she gave me all of her own. "I'm so disappointed," she said, "that I won't be in Kenya for the Pope's visit. But at least you will be able to meet him." I couldn't believe my good fortune.

A group of university students—members of the Work and their friends—were planning to serenade the Pope outside the nunciature on the evening of the reception, and they asked if I would take a program book they were making and give it to the Holy Father. It seemed a rash thing to promise, but I said I would try.

President Daniel Arap Moi declared May 6 an official holiday so that as many people as possible could welcome the Pope at the airport and line his route to the cathedral. A mood of great joy and expectation spread all over Kenya.

The day dawned sunny and bright, with festivity in the air. People cheerfully made their way to the airport on foot, by *matatu* (the most popular, and often only, means of local transport: Nissan vans that travel up and down packed with people), by bus, or by whatever available means, exchanging greetings and gesticulating as they went. I went out as early as anyone so as to make sure the Kianda girls got a good place on the airstrip.

The plane was due to touch down at 3:00 P.M., and by then the tarmac airstrip was very hot, so the whole throng of schoolchildren sitting there were suffering. I presented Pamela's card at the VIP pavilion, which was next to the presidential dais, and made my way to the reserved seat. When I got there I saw friends and acquaintances, including Nairobi's mayor, Margaret Kenyatta. She smiled at me as I took Pamela's place.

Shortly after three a silver speck appeared in the cloudless sky. As it gradually grew larger, a murmur arose from the huge crowd: "The Pope's plane!" We gazed as the plane, flanked by its Kenya Air Force escort, drew nearer and nearer. At last the great Zairean aircraft touched down, ran along the runway, and came to a standstill at the edge of the long red carpet which had been laid out to welcome the Holy Father.

President Moi and his Cabinet, as well as Church leaders and other dignitaries, stood at the foot of the steps to greet His Holiness when he came down. The door of the plane opened, and cardinals came out, and then the rest of the entourage, and finally the Pope himself. He stood at the top of the stairs, a white figure waving and greeting, while the crowd went wild, waving and shouting and dancing and singing their welcome. Then he descended the steps and knelt down and kissed the Kenyan soil.

Meanwhile the diplomats had lined up along the red

carpet to greet the Holy Father on his way to the dais. A VIP was making the introductions, so I felt that to join the line might lead to an embarrassing situation. Indeed, only the diplomats themselves were invited to the carpet, not their spouses . . .

As I stood indecisively by my chair, Margaret Kenyatta called out to me in her deep, authoritative voice, "Olga! Olga, come!" So I went, and she put me beside her. When the Pope reached us, Margaret pushed me forward and said, "The principal of Kianda College," and I was able to kiss the Holy Father's ring and bid him welcome. He looked at me, paused briefly, and made the sign of the cross on my forehead.

That evening, we were blessed with heavy rain. I was getting ready to go to the reception at the nunciature when Cuca entered my room. "A couple of students just brought this book," she said, "and asked me to make sure you take it to the Pope."

"Oh, Cuca," I cried in dismay, "it's so big! How can I give that to the Pope?"

"Just take a look," she said, handing it to me. The book was in a red velvet cover with the Pope's coat of arms embroidered on it. Inside, all the songs had been written out by hand and decorated with colored African motifs. "You can't leave that behind," she went on. "I think I have a purse that's big enough to hold it." After squeezing the book into it, we found that the purse wouldn't close. "I certainly won't pass unnoticed," I said ruefully.

The street in front of the nunciature was packed with jovial students waiting in the pouring rain to sing for the Pope when the reception was over. I realized that I was the bearer of more than just a book as I maneuvered my way into the hall with my open, outsized purse.

After the Holy Father had given his address, the hundred or so guests lined up to meet him, one by one. Dorothy Hughes, now widowed, was in front of me, looking very elegant with her Dame of Malta sash. My heart beat faster as we drew nearer to where the Pope stood. Finally my turn came.

I kissed the Pope's ring and then pulled out the program, trying to ignore the surprised expression on the nuncio's face. "Holy Father," I said, "this is from the students who are waiting outside to sing for you." He looked at the book for a moment and then handed it to his assistant. "Where are you from?" he asked. I said, "I'm from the United States, Your Holiness." His face lit up. "Ah!" he said. "United States!"

With that I felt encouraged to go on. I told him that my father was Jewish and of Polish extraction, and the Pope became very interested. It deeply impressed me that the Holy Father gave me all his attention, as if I were the only person there. I'm sure he prayed for my father while I talked about him. When he turned to greet the next person, his eyes lingered on me, as if he would have liked to prolong the conversation.

The next day the Holy Father celebrated Mass in Uhuru Park, and President Moi attended with his Cabinet. I stayed at home because we couldn't all leave the house, but I was able to watch everything on TV.

The Mass was followed by a colorful ceremony in which Pope John Paul was made a Kenyan Elder. First, several Elders presented him with the traditional symbols of authority: a beaded stool and a fly whisk. He was invited to sit on the stool and then crowned with a special colobus monkey headdress which is worn by the person who occupies the highest judiciary position in the community. The Holy Father waved the fly whisk, to the delight of the cheering crowd.

On the third day the Pope left early in the morning from Jomo Kenyatta Airport, and the scene of two days before was repeated in reverse. The Honor Guard appeared once again in full regalia (red uniforms, colobus monkey helmets), marching with perfect precision, the brass band playing. President Moi gave a short thank-you speech, and the Holy Father moved everyone with his words of farewell. "More than ever," he said, "I now feel that I belong to you. May God bless all Kenya! Till we meet again."

The Pope was accompanied by the President and his Cabinet along the red carpet to the steps of the waiting Air Zaire DC 10 which was to take him to Accra, Ghana. At the top of the stairs he turned to bless the multitude, which was singing, shouting greetings, and weeping, all at the same time. Finally he entered the plane, and a short while later it was taxiing along the runway. Then it turned away. Our last glimpse of the Pope was of a hand in white cassock, waving from the window.

On April 1, 1989, the Prelate of Opus Dei, Alvaro del Portillo, came to visit Kenya, fulfilling, as he said, a long-standing desire of the founder. In the Kenyatta International Conference Center two general get-togethers were to be held, on April 4 and 8. Around that time there was a seminar going on at Tigoni Study Center for married women of Opus Dei, and between classes they discussed how they should welcome the Father on his first visit to Africa. Mary Nyongesa, one of the first African supernumeraries, said that he must be made an Elder so that he could be speaking to his own people, and explained how this should be done.

That first get-together was due to start at 6:00 P.M., but by noon scores of women were already rehearsing songs of welcome with their drums while people began filling the seats of the main assembly hall. By 5:45 it was full, and Consolata Osiango, wearing a voluminous African dress, came out with a microphone to the middle of the aisle and urged everyone to join in the chorus of the first song. Soon the hall resounded with the strains of a Luhya song of praise to the firstborn son, "Mwana Wa Mberi."

When the Father and those accompanying him entered, the singing and drumming rose to a deafening pitch. As soon as they reached the dais, a line of women in African dresses filed up the aisle, dancing and singing, to offer gifts of fruits of the earth: pineapples, mangoes, corn, beans, tea, and coffee. The baskets were handed over and placed on the stage.

Then came the solemn ceremony of making the Father an Elder. He was presented first with a shield and a spear, signifying the Elder's readiness to defend his own; then with a fly whisk, symbol of authority; and finally with a ram, which is offered to a much respected person who cannot often be among his people. It took two men to haul the unwilling ram onto the stage. There they held it down while the Father touched it with both hands. Then he waved the fly whisk in the air as if blessing everyone, and said, "Now I am one of you!" At this there was a great outburst of applause.

The Father spoke a few words in Swahili: "Hamjambo?" (How are you all?) and "Mungu yuko nasi" (God is with us). Again there was loud applause. Then he took a piece of paper out of his pocket and read a Kikuyu proverb, "Kwa mwendwa gutiri Kirima" (No mountain is high enough to keep us from a loved one), and explained that the loved one who awaits us at the top of the mountain is Christ our Lord.

"With him everything is possible, but we have to make an effort," he said. "That is what I have come to ask of you: to make a greater effort to draw closer to God every day." Then he explained how it was that the founder of Opus Dei had chosen Kenya as the first country in which to begin the Work in Africa. It had been providential, and people often asked me how it had happened. I was glad to hear the Father speak of it now.

"After thinking about it very carefully in the presence of God," he said, "our founder chose Kenya. Then he sent his first sons and his first daughters to this country.

Since then, how many things have happened! How much work has been done! Our founder followed the apostolates of his daughters and sons in Kenya step by step. He helped them with his prayer and with his advice. He held Kenya and all of Africa deep in his heart."

The second get-together, on April 8, was still more crowded than the first, and we ran out of earphones for the translations. Families and friends of members of the Prelature had come from all over Kenya and neighboring countries to meet the Prelate of Opus Dei.

This time the Father began with a reference to the motto "Harambee!"

"You have a beautiful way of saying 'all together,' and a beautiful way of practicing it as well, with what you call 'harambee,'" he said. "Harambee! All together! That is the way we are now, all together, with thousands of people praying for you and for me; praying that you may listen to the Holy Spirit as he stirs your souls, and make up your minds to be a bit better. I know that you are good, but we all have to improve." The Father commented on how impressed he had been that morning by the sight of "rivers" of people hurrying to work in town, and spoke of the duty we have to help all people realize that their work is a way to heaven.

During the ten days he spent in Nairobi the Father visited all the centers and received many families and friends of the people of the Work.

The Kianda primary school had begun a few months before, with forty six-year-olds. On the day of his visit to the school, they waited for the Father at the door, dressed in their assembly uniform, complete with maroon cardigans and bow ties. They sang several songs for him, and one little girl presented him with a bouquet of flowers.

The Father told them, "My daughters, I pray very much for your families—for Dad and Mom, for your brothers and sisters.

"I want to remind you that the salvation of Africa lies with the woman. She is the one who works most and the one who needs to be most devout. Here you learn to relate to our Lord and to fulfill your obligations conscientiously, so that later on you will be strong women, good Christians. Make good use of the formation you receive here."

The high-school girls filled the whole courtyard of Kianda Residence, and they received the Father with drums and kayambas, singing "Jambo, jambo, Baba, karibuni Kenya" (Hello, hello, Father, welcome to Kenya).

The Father said to them, "I'm very happy that you sang that lovely welcome song. You said 'Jambo, jambo, Baba,' 'Hello, hello, Father,' and I thank you because I do love you like a father. I'm remembering the founder of Opus Dei, who gave the impulse to start Kianda College and who, while he was on earth, carried you deep inside his heart and prayed for you, being, as he was, a saint. Now from heaven he is blessing you.

"My daughters, you are here to be formed. Study hard. Receive with an open mind the advice you are given—which is not just for your personal advantage, but for you to make fructify—and so become competent, strong women filled with the spirit of God."

It is said that when someone visits Africa, they leave with nostalgia and long to return; the "call of Africa" takes hold of them. The Father told us before he left that he wouldn't be troubled by that call "because I am leaving my heart in Africa."

25

Towards a Better Life

"Frankie, how is your 'sweet journey to Rome' going?" I asked Francesca Gikandi, the principal of the Kimlea Girls' Technical Training Center in Tigoni.

She laughed. "Sweeter every day! The bees are working overtime. There are sixteen hives now and we're constantly harvesting. The containers with honey in the comb sell very well in the health food stores.

"And that's not all. The rabbit production unit is going strong, and with several laboratories we have standing orders for young rabbits. The students are making and selling biscuits, cakes, and *mandazis* [a local doughnut], and we just sold the fruit from our twenty avocado trees. An export company bought and harvested hundreds of avocados. The other day an English neighbor stopped to look at the agapanthuses that grow along our driveway, and she said, 'Would you mind selling me some? I could send a man to cut them. You see, I have an export business.' There were plenty of flowers, so that added a good bit to our income."

"So it looks like you'll be able to come for the beatification?" I asked.

"Of course!" Frankie replied. "Cuca and I calculate that we will make enough money for four of us to go from Kimlea—two teachers and two students. I wrote to my former headmistress, who has retired to their convent in Rome, and she says the nuns will be delighted to put us up in their guest wing."

"How lucky you are!" I said. "Accommodation is a real problem. They are expecting about three hundred thousand people from all over the world, including three hundred Kenyans."

In the letter that Don Alvaro wrote to us when the Father passed away on June 26, 1975, he asked us to pray and ask for prayers for "the Father who has left us, but who has not left us." He also told us we should make good use of the Father's intercession because in heaven he would be more active than ever.

Not long afterwards the prayer card for private devotion was printed, and many tens of thousands distributed all around Kenya and in neighboring countries. I never went anywhere without them because I often met people who asked for one. The prayer included a petition for the beatification of this Servant of God.

On May 17, 1992, in a memorable ceremony in St. Peter's Square, Pope John Paul II solemnly declared "Blessed" two persons: Josemaría Escrivá, priest, and Josefina Bakhita, an African Conossian nun. The immense crowd broke into prolonged applause as the pictures of the new blesseds were unveiled and the familiar figure of the Father, in black cassock, smiled down at us from the façade of St. Peter's.

The beatification was the occasion of a joyful family reunion. People came from the four corners of the earth, and I ran into many persons I hadn't seen for years. Carlette and Pim came from Holland, Charo and Joan from Nigeria (with a big group of Nigerians), and from Ireland came Teddy, Maire, and Olive, who was very amused that I still remembered her song "Come On, Come On, Come On, You Lazy Donkey!"

Eulalia Namai (née Onyango) of KBC, the producer of the Kianda Christmas programs, attended in an official capacity so that she could work with RAI (the Italian broadcasting company) and bring back a videotape for transmission in Kenya. She worked intensely both in Rome and on her return, saying, "No one should miss this!" and on May 31 the ceremony was televised for an estimated audience of one million Kenyans.

Frankie and Cuca set up accommodations in the Kimlea

Training Center for viewing by the villagers, many of whom had a devotion to Blessed Josemaría and had received favors from God through his intercession. Most were illiterate but knew the prayer by heart, in Kikuyu.

"I looked around at all those tea pickers," Cuca told me later, "their eyes glued to the television set while Frankie translated into Kikuyu, and I remembered our Father's words, 'There are people I love very much, in different parts of the world, who are doing a great work among peasant farmers through initiatives of different kinds. Their aim is not to take them away from the countryside, but to provide them with the means for living a spiritually and financially secure life, to which they have every right.' Little by little, Kimlea is changing these women's lives."

It all began when the Kianda Foundation bought a portion of Kimlea Estate, a coffee farm in Tigoni, fifteen miles outside Nairobi, for what was to become the Tigoni Study Center. Cuca helped run Kimlea, the catering side of the center, and got to know not only the neighboring farmers, but also the situation of the tea and coffee pickers on the huge estates in the area.

"They must be the most miserable people in Kenya," she said, "because they have no land anywhere. I'm reminded of Steinbeck's *Grapes of Wrath,* where the pickers were always going from one place to another to pick peaches. Landless people from all over Kenya, as well as refugees from other countries, come to these estates to earn a little money by picking. Whole families—seven or eight people—live in a single mud or timber room with no sanitary facilities. After the day's work the women fetch water from the river in *debes* [large tin containers] and carry them uphill on their backs.

"Most of the picking is done by women and children. In the peak season they work from morning to night. They're paid per kilo, and a good picker earns about a dollar a day. The families can't survive on those wages.

Men can pick faster and earn more, but they often go elsewhere in search of better jobs, so the women and children are left abandoned on the estate to survive as best they can."

The problem was huge. The fact is that over fifty percent of Kenyans live below the poverty line; only God knows how they keep body and soul together. There were all kinds of poverty alleviation programs that never seemed to get off the ground. What could we do to at least help some people?

"Education," said Cuca. "The only thing these people know how to do is pick. If they could be taught a trade, their standard of living would improve and their children could go to school and have a better start in life."

Cuca began by setting up cooking and literacy classes to be given on weekends in the garden of Kimlea. (In the rural areas, most of the cooking is done outdoors, either on the portable tin charcoal stove called a *jiko* or on a stove made of three stones and utilizing kindling and firewood.) At first the women were slow in coming. It was too much of an effort in their work-filled lives to start learning. But a few ventured around and soon discovered that the reading, writing, and arithmetic classes were of immediate practical value.

"Now I can read the number on the bus!" one woman exclaimed. Before, she had to rely on help from neighbors. Another was happy because now she could count for herself the kilos of tea she had collected and check the payment. More women began to come, and the girls also started showing interest in taking the classes. This was a big breakthrough, since they had not been very motivated.

In 1982 the Kianda Foundation put up a prefabricated building for the classes, but the numbers had grown so high that there were always some groups in the garden as well. The students were taught how to cook mandazis, cakes, and chapatis on the jiko, and soon were able to start their own little businesses. At first the client was asked to bring the ingredients, but soon the girls built up a little capital and were able to bake and sell products that were completely their own.

Joyce Wambui Waweru had been picking tea since the age of ten. One day she heard about the Kimlea adult literacy and cooking classes and decided to enroll. With her newfound skills, Joyce set up a little eatery right in the middle of the tea estates. With the proceeds she was able to send all her children, and also her younger sister, to high school. Realizing the potential of the venture, she and her husband opened a grocery store at the local shopping center and moved the family from the tea estate to a rented house in Limuru. They now have a bigger store and are building their own house. Joyce also sent her firstborn for computer training.

Joyce succeeded because she had a dream and only needed a catalyst. Not all women are like her. Some have smaller dreams and others need more help, more pushing.

Cuca and the rest of the Kimlea staff were involved in another major issue. The Ministry of Education changed the school system, adding another year to primary school and including occupational subjects so that children who couldn't continue their studies would have some skills with which to earn a living. One of the subjects that had to be taught was home economics.

The headmaster of a primary school near Kimlea came to see Cuca. "I believe you run cooking classes here," he said. "Could your teachers come a couple of times a week to our school? We have no one to teach home economics." The school had over a thousand children. Several Kimlea staff members—graduates of Kibondeni—went two afternoons a week to teach the girls. But before long they were asked to teach in eleven other schools, each with about that same number of children, which was impossible.

"We should have our own technical school," Cuca said. "Most of the families of the schoolchildren have a small plot of land. We could teach them agriculture as well as a trade that they can do at home, like tailoring, knitting, baking . . . Then they won't drift to town looking for money, which is another serious social problem."

Tere discovered that the project of a girls' technical training school had very good chances of being supported by donors overseas.

The Kianda Foundation presented a proposal to the European Community, in conjunction with an Italian nongovernmental organization, and it was approved. A good, functional building was put up for the Kimlea Girls' Technical Training Center, where ninety girls from the villages around can on a full-time basis take courses leading to recognized government trade certificates. They learn machine knitting, tailoring, agriculture, rabbit raising, beekeeping, organic farming, nutrition, cooking, and housekeeping.

Frankie Gikandi moved to Kimlea to head the new school. A Kikuyu herself, she could communicate easily with the villagers and was familiar with the environment, as she herself had grown up in a rural village in a family of fifteen children.

Starting the new school was another adventure. Cuca and Frankie moved around the countryside learning the latest agricultural techniques so that they could apply them to the Kimlea Training Center's model farm. They visited experimental farms in several places. In Ngong they learned about raising rabbits and about cultivating tomatoes and high-altitude papayas; in Lenana, about beekeeping; in Thika, about honey processing; and in Kiambu, at the Education Office, about the care of avocado trees. Soon the model farm was flourishing and the Tigoni Study Center residents benefited from its fresh, organically grown fruits and vegetables.

Inside the classrooms the students attended nutrition,

machine knitting, and tailoring classes. As soon as they started learning, they could begin small income-generating activities of their own, such as patching clothes at ten shillings a patch, and so they could earn the nominal tuition of two dollars a month. Students who had difficulties in raising cash could come and work on the shamba on weekends to pay their tuition.

"It teaches the girls responsibility and makes them value what they learn," Frankie told me. "They also put it into practice at home. Even though they have nothing, you'd be surprised at what the girls can do. I visited the home of one student and found that she had very evenly covered the walls with flattened milk cartons. It looked like wallpaper and kept out the rain.

"In the process their mothers become interested. One mother told me, 'My daughter has changed so much in the last two months. She used to be lazy and rude, and now she helps me in the house, she is clean and tidy. What do you teach here?' "

"Are you able to do anything for the mothers?" I asked.

"Yes," said Frankie, "we run courses for women on Saturdays, where we teach them sewing and cooking, and from time to time we hold seminars on family issues.

"Also we go out and teach in the villages. For the full-time program we are restricted to girls who live near enough to walk to school. But there are also hundreds of women and girls in the outlying villages who haven't had any schooling. So we set up an outreach program providing evening and weekend courses for them in their villages. Every village has a large shed which serves as an assembly hall, and we give the classes there. At present we are looking after five villages. On two week-days, after working hours, one teacher goes to each village, and on Saturdays the women come to Kimlea."

I said, "How do you teach them out in the village? They don't have sewing machines there."

"No," answered Frankie, "they sew by hand. But you'd be surprised at what the women can do. Mama Mauti wanted to make a dress for each of her twin daughters, but with eight children to feed she couldn't afford to buy the material. So she took apart one of her own skirts and learned in class how to cut the material and sew the dresses.

"The idea caught on, and now when our students at Kimlea learn how to cut material for a child's dress and use a sewing machine, they buy a large women's second-hand dress at the local market for twenty shillings, cut it, and make it up into two little dresses which sell at fifty shillings each, and the student comes out with a profit of eighty shillings."

"Do all the students find work when they finish at Kimlea?" I asked Frankie.

"Yes," she said. "They are employed in institutions and private homes, or else they start their own small businesses. Some go on to Kibondeni to continue their studies." She also told me that the Fanusi students help Kimlea in various ways.

Susan Kibue, an architecture student, designed Kimlea's school chapel, using African motifs. The women and girls have a Kikuyu priest of Opus Dei to attend to their spiritual needs. The advent of African priests has brought a new dynamism and authenticity to the Work in Africa.

Don Alvaro spoke about the first African priests of Opus Dei during one of the get-togethers in the Kenyatta International Conference Center in 1989. "I remember," he said, "how moved the founder of Opus Dei was when, many years ago, the first African women went to Rome to receive formation there and one of them said to him that she was praying, and was offering up her work and the difficulties of learning a new language, for the future African priests of the Work. . . . I assure you that our founder was very moved. He repeated it often, full of holy pride, because it was the Holy Spirit who had made this daughter of his pray for the future vocations of African priests, which are now a reality."

There are now five Kenyan priests of Opus Dei: Father Paul Mimbi, from Mombasa, ordained in 1982 by Pope John Paul II; Father Anthony Muheria, from Murang'a, ordained in 1993 by the first Prelate of Opus Dei, Bishop Alvaro del Portillo; Father Gabriel Mureithi, from Nyeri, ordained in 1995 by the present Prelate, Bishop Javier Echevarría; and Fathers Luigino Miungi, from Meru, and Silvano Ochuodo, from Ugenya, both ordained in 1998 by Bishop Echevarría. Formerly they were all engineers except for Father Mureithi, who was a forester.

Kimlea is doing the difficult but vital job of changing the poorest and most disadvantaged of girls—girls who would otherwise fall prey to all kinds of things. Already this work is having an impact and showing that no one is too deprived to be helped to put meaning, hope, and a little security in their life.

The Kimlea Training Center is involved not only in education, but in anything that will help make people's lives a little better and easier. It has helped the parents of a severely disabled eighteen-year-old girl who for years had been kept hidden in the house. She started getting sunshine, proper exercise, and home nursing, and now she takes her limited part in family life. A Good Samaritan has given her a wheelchair so that the family can move her around more easily.

Three orphaned siblings have been put under appropriate care.

The staff at Kimlea are trying hard to put into practice the teaching of Blessed Josemaría, "We have to uphold the right of all men to live, to own what is necessary to lead a dignified existence, to work and to rest, to choose a particular state in life, to form a home, to bring children into the world within marriage and to be allowed to educate them, to pass peacefully through times of sickness and old age, to have access to culture, to join with other citizens to achieve legitimate ends, and, above all, the right to know and love God in perfect liberty" (*Friends of God*, no. 171).

✻ 26 ✻

Kibondeni College

One day in March 1998 I entered my office to find on the desk a little roll of parchment, tied with gold string, addressed to me. It was an invitation, handwritten in silver script, to the "Nairobi Summit" of an international congress on "Tradition and Innovation: In Search of a New Equilibrium for the Service Sector in the Third Millennium." Organized by Kibondeni College, this conference was to take place in the Silver Room of the Hilton Hotel on Saturday, March 28. The guest of honor was to be Professor Julia Gitobu, Dean of the Faculty of Home Economics at Kenyatta University.

I telephoned the principal of Kibondeni, Berni Okondo. Berni had followed her sister Ursula to Kianda College in the 1960s and then gone into the catering profession. Like Ursula, she had also joined Opus Dei, and for the last twenty years had been involved in the running of Kibondeni.

"I just received your beautiful invitation, and I'm most impressed," I told her.

"Don't miss the occasion!" she said, laughing off the compliment. "The students have been preparing for it for months, six other colleges are participating, and the nine winning research papers are really good."

"What are they about?" I asked.

"Everything from outside catering to care of the sick. The students have done research showing how traditional and innovative methods can be combined to give more personalized services. They feel that the new millennium should see society more concerned about the person receiving the service than about technological advancement. Traditional modes of hospitality and ways of showing solidarity with the sick and suffering should not be lost. Come—you'll find it very interesting."

"I certainly will," I replied, thinking how far the training school—now Kibondeni College—had come since the days of the first six Kikuyu girls in 1961, when no one believed that African women could do this kind of work.

The Strathmore College students had been the first to appreciate the quality of the services provided by the catering department. A friend of mine from Nairobi University, Margaret Gachii, married one of the first Strathmore students, Peter W. Muthoka. Now a business executive, he proudly calls himself a "founder student" of Strathmore.

"Strathmore College prepared me for life," he once said to me. "Not only academically, but also socially. Like most of the other African students, I came from a rural environment, and the way we were looked after at the college was an eye-opener for me. Our clothes were laundered and mended for us, our rooms were cleaned, and we had four meals a day (breakfast, lunch, tea, and dinner), sharing tables with the teachers. We learned courtesy and good manners from all this, and how to behave in a well-run home. I wanted my own home to run in that smooth way, and my wife and I worked together to create a disciplined home atmosphere for our children. Good living habits stay with you and have a positive, multiplying effect on society."

The first six Kikuyu girls were soon followed by young women from other tribes all over the country, and within two years the number had increased to thirty. As time went by, people became more and more aware of the potential of the catering profession. It is, as Berni puts it, "extremely marketable."

By 1967 Kibondeni was offering its own certificates, with the authorization of the Nairobi City Council. When the Ministry of Science and Technology was formed in 1975, Kibondeni applied for recognition of its three-year program and curriculum. No such program had yet been registered, but on account of its record and years of experience, Kibondeni was asked to collaborate in putting together the curriculum which would be used by all future catering schools. The exams are given by the Kenya National Examinations Council. For the first three years Kibondeni was the only college to present candidates. Now there are dozens of catering schools all over the country.

At first all the students were drawn from among primary school leavers whose parents could not afford the tuition for secondary school. The girls boarded at the catering school and paid for their studies with practical work they did for the college, receiving a little pocket money as well. But as time went on, parents were better able to pay tuition for secondary school, and Kibondeni raised the standard of admission from primary school leavers to secondary school leavers.

"We have to do something, though, for the primary school leavers," said Berni. "Without some form of training they will be lost." And so in 1987 the program was expanded to include a two-year crafts course for girls of this level.

If Kianda College has a network of alumnae working all over Kenya, the same can be said for Kibondeni. Its four thousand alumnae work in institutions and homes, including their own, in many parts of the country, where they exercise an incredible influence in raising standards. Even the trainees make an impact when they go out for their yearly industrial attachment.

Cleaning, maintenance, and repairs are a real problem in institutions all over the country—a problem that Kibondeni is trying to tackle through the training given to the students. From the stories Berni tells, they seem to be gaining ground.

Two trainees were taken on for their industrial attachment by the Esperia Hotel in Westlands. They spent the first week thoroughly scrubbing the kitchen. When the manager appeared a few days later, he looked around and then asked the department head, "Who authorized the painting of those two stoves?" The man grinned and replied, "They haven't been painted. Those girls scrubbed them till the blue came up!" As a result the manager employed two alumnae, one to head the laundry and housekeeping department, and the other to run the kitchen and restaurant.

The Kibondeni girls on attachment at the Impala Hotel began cleaning the rooms the way they had been taught, taking the carpets outside for beating, and removing mattresses from the beds to dust the springs. "They filled buckets with fluff!" exclaimed Berni. "The manager saw them carry them out, and he asked where all that dust had come from. When they told him, he was both surprised and pleased. He said, 'I never thought that bedsprings needed to be cleaned!'"

Mena Imbosa went to work in a huge school in western Kenya where the menu was corn and beans every day except Sunday, when there was rice with "soup" (broth). The food was dished out onto plates and the boys ate wherever they could around the compound. There was a huge assembly hall, but it had no chairs. The hall was caked with grime. As high as the arm could reach, there were fingerprints, and above that, thick cobwebs where spiders had lived undisturbed for many years.

Mena began by carefully calculating costs to see where she could save in order to vary the diet. Soon she was serving other vegetables at the meals, and meat twice a week, on the same amount of money and even with some left over at the end of the month. She asked the principal if he could put that money aside to be used later. After six months the amount was substantial and she used it to paint the hall. Six months later she bought benches and tables so that the boys now had a dining hall. They were delighted.

Before the inauguration of the dining hall, the school board provided funds for painting the outside of it, and under the inscription and date they wrote the name of the cateress who had made it possible.

Then there is Emily Wangesi, who went to work for a hospital. Soon she realized that there was pilfering going on. As she was directing a team of men and they were much older than she was, Emily thought, "I must go about this very carefully." Not long afterwards she discovered that these men were working on Sundays. She asked them, "Don't you go to church?" They replied, "How can we, since we have to work?" "All right," she said, "we'll make a roster. You each take two hours, so that everyone can go to his church." They did that, to everyone's satisfaction, and later they talked about what the respective priest or minister had said.

"This is the right moment to tackle the pilfering," Emily thought. So she said to the men, "Now we're all going to church and you discuss good things. But how is it that at the same time sugar, flour, milk, and rice are disappearing from the kitchen? That doesn't make sense." The men shook their heads and answered sheepishly, "You're right, it is true." And the things stopped disappearing. But Emily felt she should do something for the men, since they really needed it. So she went to talk to the management. "Couldn't we give them some food every week," she asked, "so that they don't feel like stealing it?" The idea met with approval, and now every worker is given a packet of food to take home each week. The management trusts its people so much that they are the ones who receive and sign for the goods.

A couple of Kibondeni girls on attachment in a school in Nyeri found the kitchen extremely dirty, so they made a roster for special cleaning. Each worker had a portion of the kitchen to clean every day until, by the end of the week, it was perfectly clean. They also suggested that sawdust be placed outside the dining hall to prevent the students from tracking mud into it.

One day the headmaster announced that the Minister of Education was coming to the school. This meant cleaning and decorating the dining hall, carrying chairs, and other chores. The girls invited the senior boys to their house for tea and explained to them how much their help was needed for the hall, and how they had thought that the bins could be wrapped in colored paper and filled with flowers. The boys collaborated wholeheartedly, and on the day the Minister arrived the hall was beautiful. "I've never seen flowers in this hall before!" said the delighted headmaster. Moreover, it was the first time anyone had seen senior boys cleaning. After that it became a tradition for seniors to decorate the hall on special occasions. The two girls, meanwhile, were given permanent employment in the school.

Kibondeni was given the honor of being asked to bake the cake for the centennial of St. Austin's Church, which took place on May 23, 1999. The event drew visitors from all over the world. It was a great occasion, marking the first one hundred years of Catholicism in Nairobi. A congregation of more than six thousand was expected, and there needed to be enough cake to go around. Mildred Okutu, a numerary assistant, designed the cake, and it took a week to make. It was enormous. It looked like a big train, occupying the length of three whole walls! It had on it different motifs: Mount Kenya; a model of the church, complete with steeple, door, and windows; coffee plants and beans (recalling the farm of St. Austin's that was started by the Holy Ghost Fathers in 1899) . . . all done in icing. It had to be wheeled away and displayed on a wagon! But it was greatly admired and enjoyed by all. Not a crumb was wasted, and the "church" was rescued and carried away to be enjoyed in peace by the Holy Ghost Fathers and their friends. The parish priest, Father Patrick Leonard, wrote to thank

Kibondeni for the "beautiful and magnificent cake," saying that it was "a real show of workmanship and an honor to the parish and the Christians who attended the Mass."

Due to the quality of the teaching and facilities at Kibondeni, the Ministry encouraged the management to start a diploma program. However, they put this off, because they wanted to continue helping girls whose education had been cut short for lack of tuition money. But as the situation improved and more parents were able to pay tuition, junior high graduates with good grades applied, and so in 1998 the diploma program was introduced and the Kibondeni School of Institutional Management became Kibondeni College.

I thought of all these things as I parked the car and walked across Mama Ngina Street towards the Hilton Hotel, along with many other people. We were met in the grand foyer by stylish-looking Kibondeni students, wearing yellow sashes, who directed us up the carpeted stairs to the Silver Room, where we were invited to sign the visitors' book before proceeding to the rapidly filling plush seats facing the dais and speakers' podium.

The Summit brought together distinguished persons from such Nairobi catering institutions as Utalii College, Virginia Slims, and the Kenya Institute of Catering, and it was impressive to see the many young people gathered there, eager to make a contribution towards improving hospitality skills.

Professor Gitobu commented that she had attended many top-level presentations and research-paper readings, but had rarely seen them so well produced, and she congratulated the young people on their work. During her speech, she also announced a new "tourism and hotelier" degree that Kenyatta University will soon be offering.

Kibondeni College aims at reaching this top level one day, and thanks to the generosity of Mrs. Dorothy

Hughes, we already have the site for the new campus. It will soon be a reality, although, sadly, Dorothy is no longer here to rejoice with us over it.

Six Times Ten

"Mrs. Hughes, do you realize what you are doing?" asked the lawyer in a stern voice, nervously wringing his hands.

Dorothy, who was in the chair directly across from him, turned to look at Tere and me. We were in his office, where she had called us for a meeting. She was a woman who knew her mind—a confident and decisive person, not sentimental but steadfastly levelheaded.

"Yes," she said firmly. "I want the Kianda Foundation to have my house for the education of Kenyan women and girls. It's too big for me to look after alone, and the children are all settled elsewhere." She did not mention that what she was about to pass on to us was a prime piece of property, a jewel, practically invaluable.

We called the house "Glenview," and the Regional Advisory moved there while the Kianda Foundation got ready to build a new Kibondeni College campus on the property. The college would now train girls to the highest levels of catering and of institutional management, offering degrees in these essential fields.

Glenview is a lovely place. The office where I work has windows overlooking the tree-lined driveway, the sunken gardens, and two palm trees that have grown so tall that they are long trunks with tufts on top—a testimony to the passing of time. The office also has sliding glass doors that rattle when they're opened.

Tere slid them open one evening and stood in the doorway, looking very pale. Little veins on her lined forehead were standing out. "Olga, I'm just so tired," she said limply. "I don't know what's the matter with me."

There was something the matter. Tere had a heart

condition. The doctors prescribed that she leave Nairobi, because of its high altitude, and return to Spain.

That was in 1991. Tere left a deep furrow behind her. She had been a pillar of strength, a practical person who knew how to translate a dream into reality. I missed her very much.

Then came the momentous day when Kianda closed as a college, leaving only the school. The time had come to move on. "Kianda will never be the same," mourned Dorina, as she and Celia Donovan packed the last items of furniture into the van which would take them to the new location in Madaraka, an area on the south side of Nairobi, where the secretarial college was going to form part of the Strathmore Post-Secondary Educational College. "Kianda was always so homey," she said. "Everyone knew everyone else. Now everything will be different."

It *was* different. Nairobi had entered the technological age, and new demands were being made on the management and secretarial staff which couldn't be met by the limited resources of the old Kianda. The secretarial section of Strathmore College would take double the number of students and offer the best in computer technology.

At Strathmore the students are properly equipped for entry into the competitive business world. Also, in an attempt to stem the tide towards professional ineptitude and corruption, the college is making plans for a department of professional ethics. And plans are quite advanced for Strathmore to become a university.

Not long after the move, Dorina came home and said, "I don't know what we're going to do. The college chapel is to be dedicated next month, and the artist painting the altarpiece has walked off the job. More than half the reredos are unfinished, and some haven't even been started!"

Immediately I thought of Brigid. "I wonder if my artist sister would be willing to come out from England and finish those paintings," I mused.

"Oh, do you really think she might?" Dorina asked, brightening. "I think that's a wonderful idea!" So did everyone else, and the management offered to bring her out to do the painting.

I telephoned Brigid. She was very surprised to be invited for such a big job and at such short notice, but she loves a challenge, and so she came to Nairobi to take charge of the situation. This was in November of 1994. She spent two weeks on top of scaffolding in the Strathmore chapel, completing all the unfinished paintings and adding new ones.

She cheerfully incorporated all the suggestions made to her, and from time to time enlisted the help of college students, including one young man who patiently posed for her painting of the bare feet of the kneeling Christ in the Agony in the Garden. Brigid was careful to keep to the original artist's inspiration, and commented that his work was very good. Everyone was pleased with the end result and very grateful to Brigid.

My sister and I attended together the solemn Mass inaugurating the chapel, and she was pleased to see how the beautiful reredos dominated the sanctuary. On either side hung a painting she had made: on one side, a full-length portrait of Blessed Josemaría in his monsignor's cape, and on the other, the guardian angel of the Work. The Father seemed to be smiling down at the congregation that spilled out of the chapel that morning.

Brigid's visit to Nairobi coincided with my sixtieth birthday, and she came laden with gifts from my parents and sisters in England, while my brothers sent letters from across the Atlantic. John even composed a poem:

Sonnet to Olga

(Tetrameter after our great-aunt Edna St. Vincent Millay)

Only diamonds wear so hard,
Long years reflected and polished clear.
Grafton Street memories loose now are jarred,

And Dublin's fair city in the '50's, so dear.
Mercury, Saturn, Venus, Mars:
Africa seemed such a long way away,
Replete with giraffes, but very few cars . . .
Little we knew of Kianda's great way.
In earnest deciding, our paths we took,
Nairobi-ward Olga, and I to New York.
I thought about Olga when Trade Centers
    shook:
She knew what mattered when she chose her
    fork.
6 times 10 have sped the decades!
O cry alleluia! ere memory fades.

I was moved, and amazed at how swiftly the years had passed. But they were years filled with work, the joy of friendship, and God's renewing love. And in the meantime my little brother had grown up!

Brigid and I decided to prepare a surprise for our parents. We recorded several of the songs from our youth, singing them in harmony, and Brigid brought the tape back to London with her. Soon afterwards Mother wrote me this letter:

Dearest Olletje,
May I congratulate you on your 60th birthday? Some people would not want to be congratulated— but that is foolishness. God has given you life—and more abundantly. I look forward to my 87th. If God keeps us alive, it is because we fulfill a necessary function. And Brigid tells me the work you are doing is marvelous. How proud I am of my family, and how humble I feel. . . .

When I first saw Daddy (though I only saw his back), I felt God was whispering to me, "This is the one I selected for you." There were times when it was difficult—as you know—but he was God's choice and that made a big difference to me! I left it all to him, and now Daddy is so gentle and so generous; so wise with the grandchildren—so interested in all the ways of life and studies. God has indeed brought me into fertile pasture. How stupid anyone who refuses a child. What riches in each one! And what a wonderful thing to share.

Brigid is just back and told us of all her experiences and the dangers and difficulties of her work, and the success, and the rejoicing, and the Mass that was celebrated in the Strathmore chapel. When the altarpiece I'm doing is finished, will you have Mass in front of it too?

I loved your singing all the old favorites—how memories fly back, and what happy ones! Ours was really a little Eden, a family that loved, and that is a warm thankfulness in my heart. . . .

I hear a lot from the boys now. John is giving me a booksigning party—I'll be in New York from the 15th to the 22nd of December. He is very excited about it, and we'll see a rehearsal of his play. He went to lectures about "Marriage in the Middle Ages" and he was very impressed. "In those days," he told me over the phone, "people weren't looking for power, but for love." And after some reflection: "I think we're in such a bad way because we've turned our back on God." . . .

You are a rich element in my life, though I don't see you often!

A big, big hug,
Your Mother and Father

But Mother didn't get to New York. At the beginning of December Brigid telephoned and told me in a trembling voice, "Olgie—Daddy has had an accident and is unconscious. Liz has put him in the best hospital, and Mother is with him all the time . . ." I put down the receiver and sat stunned, trying to imagine what was happening in a London hospital. I knew that my father suffered from Parkinson's disease, but he had been coping well. I prayed for Daddy with all my heart.

My father never regained consciousness. On December 12, while Kenya was celebrating Uhuru Day, Johnny telephoned from London to tell me that Daddy had passed away. "I'm sorry to be the one to have to break the news to you," he said, a lump in his voice.

I flew to London as soon as I could and went straight to my parents' home. The potted white lilies from Daddy's funeral were on the porch, still blooming. After the service, John had flown with Daddy's body to New York. Daddy was buried beside his parents, as he had wished.

Everything in the house looked just the same, with my father's coats and hats hanging in the hall and his briefcases standing under the staircase. It was a poignant reminder of his absence, and I buried my face in one of those coats and wept. I enfolded Mother in my arms, in a wordless embrace. She was still in shock, but consoled at having her six children around her.

We celebrated New Year's Eve in Sheila's home and New Year's Day with Liz, and everyone covered Mother with attentions, while drawing comfort from one another.

Brigid had to put the final touches to her work at Strathmore College, so she suggested that Mother accompany her to have a complete change. I was also happy at the thought of having her near me during that time.

At the end of our last evening together in Berkhamsted, I accompanied Liz to her car and asked her, "What is the best thing to do for Mother? How can I help her?" and she answered gravely, "It's like an amputation. It will take months for Mother to get over it."

Mother and Brigid spent two weeks in Nairobi. While Brigid painted at Strathmore, Mother sat in the sunny garden of Glenview making lovely watercolor pictures of astramanias for the living room of Samara, the new teacher's house at Kianda School. The last altarpiece she painted, one of the Virgin and Child surrounded by little angels of all races, hangs in the Samara chapel, and Mass is often said in front of it, as she wished.

My mother is an extraordinary woman in all ways. Recently she underwent a hip replacement, at ninety-one. A couple of weeks after the surgery she exclaimed, full of high spirits, "I am no longer a human being, I am a hymn of praise!" Indeed she is. I am fortunate to have been able to borrow the song of my life from this magnificent hymn.

Epilogue

"Dream, and your dreams will fall short," Blessed Josemaría Escrivá used to tell us. It was his way of expressing his conviction that all human activities could be raised to the level of the divine. He gave his spiritual sons and daughters a vision of the world that inspired them to use their creative energies to draw the many aspects of human endeavor to God, working side by side with their fellow men and women.

He had a broad and sure vision of the role women have to play in the world and in the Church. He visualized them working in all the professions, in the hurly-burly of political and business life as well as in the career of creating homes, so necessary to the happiness and well-being of families and society.

I met Opus Dei providentially in Ireland, nearly forty-five years ago, and was swept up in the vision of the founder. A few years later, in the luggage of my teacher training and, more importantly, the spirit of the Work, which I had learned from the founder, I brought a seedling to Africa, little suspecting where it would fall and into what it would grow.

When thirty-nine years ago I first came to Africa, I came with a dream which has turned into the magnificent reality of people from all walks of life, in Kenya, using their work as a means of getting closer to God and a way of serving others, opening up for them the fullness of the reality of their being children of God.

From Kenya, women have gone to help start the Work in Nigeria, the Ivory Coast, the Congo, Cameroon, and Uganda. There are wonderful young people dreaming dreams—people like Speranza Migue, whose eyes shine as she prepares to start the Work with women in South Africa.

"We black people feel that God has forgotten us," a South African friend told me sadly some months ago. How the fatherly heart of Blessed Josemaría would yearn to remedy that situation, I thought then. Now six young women are packing their bags, eager to open a center in Johannesburg: a Kenyan, a Nigerian, two Filipinas, a South American, and a European.

I wrote this book at Strathmore, where I hadn't lived since 1967. One day two trainees knocked shyly at my door and said, "Will you come to the get-together and tell us about the beginnings?" I went, and told a spellbound group of youngsters some of the things I have written here. The following morning I received a little note from Janet Mawe, saying, "When I see people like you who are old in the Work and are happy, it gives me an impression that if God wants me there, I will also be happy." She's right.

I must say that I'm happier every day and more and more grateful for the gift of my vocation, which, though undeserved, continues to fulfill me in every way. I've never for a moment regretted the decision I made at twenty. From the first fervor of my youthful enthusiasm it has attained the warmth of glowing embers that will never die out.

"Through the world still echoes that divine cry: 'I have come to cast fire upon the earth, and what will I but that it be kindled?' . . . Don't you want to spread the blaze?" (*The Way*, no. 801).